First Edition

triumphlearning™

Common Core Coach

English Language Arts 4

Assessments

Common Core Coach Assessments, English Language Arts, First Edition, Grade 4
T103NAA

ISBN-13: 978-1-61997-455-5

Cover Design: Q2A/Bill Smith
Cover Illustration: Jing Jing Tsong

Triumph Learning® 136 Madison Avenue, 7th Floor, New York, NY 10016

© 2013 Triumph Learning, LLC
Buckle Down and Coach are imprints of Triumph Learning

Printed in the United States of America.

10 9 8 7 6 5 4 3 2 1

Contents

Benchmark Assessment 1

Part 1: Reading Comprehension

Read the story and answer the questions that follow.

Chung Remains Champ

When I woke, it seemed like an ordinary day. Actually, it seemed like a beautiful day. Birds were singing, and sunlight streamed into my room. But I was scared. Today would be the final match of the table tennis tournament. In that match, I would be facing reigning table tennis champ Lee Chung.

Who would have guessed that I, Samuel Myers, would make it to the finals this year? I had never even made it to the quarterfinals before! But, as my coach pointed out, both my speed and my overall game had gotten much better.

My outlook was getting better, too. As I got dressed and ate breakfast, I put my fear aside. I began imagining the start of the game itself. I needed to act like a winner. When I walked up to the table, I would be calm. I would stare directly at Lee Chung and smile. I would wave at the crowd.

Later that morning, I did just as I had imagined. I walked calmly up to the table. I smiled at Lee. I waved at the crowd, and the crowd cheered. Listening to the applause, I thought that the reality was even better than I had imagined. Yes, I can do this, I told myself. And so the match began.

I won the first serve, which got me off to a great start. In table tennis, a good serve is hard to return, and over the past year I've developed a pretty mean serve. Before long, I was up 4–0! The look on Lee's face was getting grimmer and grimmer. I figured I was in for some tough shots.

Boy, was I right! At this point, the game seemed to speed up. My heart pounded faster than the ball zipping back and forth, and my hands were sweaty. Yet, I was able to keep up with it. In fact, the excitement of keeping up with the ball was thrilling! In the end, I hit a smash and won the first game!

To win the match, however, I had to win two games—and I lost the second game. The funny thing is, Lee looked even grimmer now than he did at the beginning of the first game, when he was losing. His brow was furrowed, and his lips were thin, pressed together tightly. Meanwhile, I felt like a nervous wreck.

I reminded myself of my calm and the audience's applause before the match. Yes, you can do this, I reminded myself. You can do this, I thought, and *Wham!* I returned Lee's next serve for a point. You can do this, I thought, and *Smash!* I served to Lee for another point! You can do this, I thought again and again until the score was 10–9 in my favor. With one more point, the match would be mine.

Then it happened. The ball started bouncing in weird ways. I thought it would go here, and it went there. I thought it would go there, and it went here. At last, I was seeing it: the Chung spin I had heard so much about. It had me swinging at a ball that was never where I thought it should be!

Before I knew it, the game and the match were over. Lee Chung was champ again. An enormous smile replaced the frown on his face. "Awesome game," he said, shaking my hand.

It *was* awesome, I realized. I smiled back at Lee. "See you next year," I said.

1. Which BEST describes the setting at the beginning of the story?

    A. It shows that Samuel is happy.

    B. It frightens Samuel.

    C. It makes Samuel believe he will win.

    D. It does not match Samuel's feelings.

2. Why is the audience's applause important to the story?

    A. It gives Samuel confidence.

    B. It shows that the crowd likes Lee better.

    C. It makes Samuel nervous.

    D. It angers Lee.

3. Read this sentence from the story.

    The funny thing is, Lee looked even grimmer now than he did at the beginning of the first game, when he was losing.

    What is the MOST LIKELY reason Lee appears "grimmer" at this stage of the game?

    A. Lee doesn't think he has any chance of winning.

    B. Lee realizes that he must win the next game, so the stakes are much higher.

    C. Lee is having trouble serving his famous "Chung spin."

    D. Lee realizes Samuel is a much better player than he previously thought.

4. Which word BEST describes Samuel at the end of the story?

    A. disappointed

    B. relieved

    C. determined

    D. calm

5. Why does Samuel say, "See you next year," to Lee Chung after the match? Explain how this statement shows that Samuel has changed from the beginning of the story.

    _____

    _____

    _____

    _____

    _____

Read the story and answer the questions that follow.

Swept Away!

Tony Ramos was in shock. One minute, he was in shallow water, diving under a wave. The next thing he knew, he was way out beyond the breakers. Fighting panic, he began swimming steadily toward shore. But when he lifted his head to get a fix on the beach, he saw that he was even farther out than before!

"Am I going crazy?" he muttered. "This can't be happening!" His heart hammering in his chest, he began to tread water. Trying to calm himself, he thought back to just a half hour earlier, in his aunt's kitchen.

Tony was washing up after his breakfast when Aunt Blanca walked into the kitchen. "Well, you're up early," she said, her brown eyes twinkling. "I suppose my Miguelito is fast asleep."

"Yeah, Mike isn't going anywhere soon," Tony said. He was staying with his aunt and cousin for two weeks. He always liked seeing them. It didn't hurt that they lived just a block from a fantastic beach.

"I see you're in your swim trunks. You aren't thinking of taking an early morning swim by yourself, are you?" asked Aunt Blanca. "Because that would be a bad idea, Antonio."

Tony put the clean cereal bowl in the cupboard, his back to his aunt as he lied. "No," he said casually. "I just thought I'd go for a walk while the beach is empty."

"Well, that's good. No one should go swimming alone. The sea is filled with surprises, and not all of them are good."

"I'll play it safe!" Tony called back, strolling out the door. But he was thinking, *I can handle myself; I'm a strong swimmer. I know how to catch the waves and take them in.*

When he got to the beach, he kicked off his sandals and sprinted into the surf. He dived under an enormous wave and came up to find himself swept out to sea—and terrified.

Now Tony began determinedly to swim to shore, at a sharper angle than before. Again he checked his position, and again, he was stunned. He was even farther out!

Trying to puzzle things out, he remembered a TV documentary about people getting caught in a bizarre current called a riptide. It pulled them out to sea even as they tried to swim to shore.

"I'm in a riptide!" he exclaimed and shivered. Many people drown in riptides every year.

To get out of this current, he should swim parallel to shore, not toward shore, he reasoned.

He began swimming again, but his strength was fading. Gasping for air, he checked his position. He was still the same distance from shore, so he was out of the current! But Tony was still a long way from the beach. And he knew with a sickening certainty that he was too exhausted to swim any farther.

His tired brain remembered a survival <u>technique</u> he'd learned in his swimming lessons: If no one is around to help you get to shore, float on your back. The waves will eventually take you in, although you'll come in much farther down the beach.

Tony flipped onto his back, greedily sucking in oxygen. He'd have to be careful about waves sloshing over his head. He was so weak, swallowing any more water just might finish him off.

As he kept alert for rough waves, Tony gazed at the blue sky and listened to the gentle lapping of the water. The world was a beautiful place, and he was grateful to be able to enjoy it. He would have a long walk when he finally got to shore—plenty of time to figure out how to apologize to his aunt, for both his stupidity and his lie.

Plenty of time, too, to think about how he had almost drowned in his recklessness.

6. Which tells what <u>technique</u> means as it is used in this story?

    A. a way of remembering

    B. a way of learning

    C. a way of swimming

    D. a way of using a skill

7. Which sentence from the story shows why Tony decides to go swimming alone?

    A. "It didn't hurt that they lived just a block from a fantastic beach."

    B. "The sea is filled with surprises, and not all of them are good."

    C. "'I just thought I'd go for a walk while the beach is empty.'"

    D. "*I can handle myself; I'm a strong swimmer.*"

8. Which word BEST describes Tony at the end of the story?

    A. sorry

    B. scared

    C. shocked

    D. happy

9. Which sentence BEST states the theme of this story?

    A. Lying always results in trouble.

    B. Swimming in the ocean is never safe.

    C. Recklessness can put you in terrible danger.

    D. TV documentaries provide useful information.

10. Write a summary of "Swept Away!"

_____

_____

_____

_____

Use "Chung Remains Champ" and "Swept Away!" to answer questions 11–12.

11. Identify the points of view used in each story. What kinds of details does each narrator share?

_____

_____

_____

_____

12. What do Samuel and Tony learn about self-confidence? Compare and contrast the lessons they learn by the end of their stories.

_____

_____

_____

_____

Read the story and answer the questions that follow.

Evangeline's Laughter

Not too long ago, but just long enough, in the little town of Peachtree, Georgia, there lived the tallest girl you've ever seen. Her name was Evangeline. By her sixteenth birthday, she was taller than the tallest tree in town.

Everyone adored Evangeline, although she often couldn't do things the usual way. But her teacher always found a way to include her. She would say, "Today we will have class outside, in the shade of the willow tree." Or before lunch, she might suggest, "Why don't we *all* wash our hands in the lake now?"

Evangeline took great pride in what she could do for her family and town. She kept her family's chimney squeaky clean and dusted the school's rooftop bell every Friday afternoon.

There's something else you should know about Evangeline. She loved to laugh so hard that tears would roll down her face. The more she laughed, the more those tears would roll.

One evening, during a bonfire party, Evangeline frolicked across the peach orchards with her classmates. As she rolled in the grass, ripe peaches fell and bonked her on the head. But Evangeline just laughed and licked away the sweet juices, giant tears rolling down her face. The tears dripped onto the bonfire and immediately put it out.

Word spread about Evangeline's firefighting ability. One afternoon, a telephone call came from the Chicago Fire Department. "Ms. Evangeline, we want you to be a member of our firefighting team."

Without hesitation, Evangeline answered, "Here I come!" She packed up her bags, which were as big as city buses, and made her way from tiny Peachtree to vast Chicago.

When she arrived, the firefighters gave Evangeline her very own hippopotamus-sized dalmatian dog, whom she named Teeny. When Teeny saw Evangeline, she jumped up and put her paws on Evangeline's shoulders. Evangeline laughed so much that her tears washed the firehouse floor.

One Sunday while playing catch in the park, Teeny kept jumping up to give Evangeline kisses. In her excitement, Teeny wagged her tail faster than a fan, and before you could say, "Wabash!" every barbecue fire in the park went out! For years after that day, the duo laughed and wagged out fires all over Chicago.

Then one summer, Evangeline heard that people out west needed help. She packed up her bags and Teeny, too, and said good-bye to her firefighter friends.

As the two traveled, Evangeline played catch with Teeny, who'd chase the ball, wagging her tail faster than a hummingbird's wings. After a while, though, Teeny seemed all tuckered out. Evangeline worried that the journey was too much, so she let Teeny rest whenever she was tired. But with Teeny resting so much, not many fires got out.

A few days later, however, Evangeline noticed that Teeny's belly was swollen. "Oh, Teeny!" Evangeline exclaimed. "You're going to have puppies!" And with that, Evangeline scooped up Teeny and crossed the Mississippi River with one giant step.

As forest fires raged in Utah, Evangeline feared she would lose all her laughter in her worry about the puppies to come. But then, she found Teeny hunkered down in the shadow of a rock in Monument Valley.

"They're here!" Evangeline cried. And sure enough, nestled up to Teeny were four dalmatian puppies, each as big as a pony. Evangeline picked up one of them, and it licked her nose with its soft, pink tongue. As Evangeline remembered Teeny's first kisses in Chicago, tears began to flow down her cheeks. She got so many kisses that afternoon that she not only put out hundreds of forest fires, she also created the Great Salt Lake.

After that, Evangeline, Teeny, and the puppies traveled on, rescuing hikers, extinguishing fires in California, and putting out volcanoes in Hawaii and Japan. Last we heard, they had been spotted playing hide-and-seek in the Himalayan Mountains.

13. Why is it important to the story that Evangeline and Teeny leave Chicago and head west?

   A. There are more fires in Utah than in Chicago.

   B. Evangeline finds more space in the west than she does in the city.

   C. People out west appreciate Evangeline's talents more.

   D. Their move west explains how Evangeline creates the Great Salt Lake.

14. Which word means the same as <u>vast</u> as it is used in this story?

   A. large

   B. noisy

   C. far away

   D. exciting

15. Which sentence from the story BEST shows Evangeline's confidence in herself?

   A. "One evening, during a bonfire party, Evangeline frolicked across the peach orchards with her classmates."

   B. "Without hesitation, Evangeline answered, 'Here I come!'"

   C. "She packed up her bags and Teeny, too, and said good-bye to her firefighter friends."

   D. "She got so many kisses that afternoon that she not only put out hundreds of forest fires, she also created the Great Salt Lake."

16. Which sentence BEST states the theme of this story?

   A. Laughter cures all problems.

   B. Being different is hardly a problem.

   C. The taller, the better.

   D. A dog is a girl's best friend.

17. Describe one event in the story that shows how important Teeny is to Evangeline. What does this event show about their relationship?

_____

_____

_____

_____

Read the story and answer the questions that follow.

Pecos Bill

Do you know how the Grand Canyon came to be? Well, here's the *true* story of how Pecos Bill and a tornado made that huge canyon in Arizona.

Now, Pecos Bill was not just anybody. He was a cowboy—and he was the best one the world has ever seen.

When Bill was just a little baby, his pa packed up the whole family in a wagon, and they headed out west.

Near the Pecos River, the wagon hit a big bump. Little Bill was thrown from the wagon, but no one even knew he had fallen out. A mama coyote found the boy, though, and she decided to raise him along with her coyote pups.

Little Bill had a fine time growing up wild with the coyotes. He spent his nights hunting and howling at the moon. However, he soon realized that he wanted to grow up not to be a coyote, but a cowboy! In fact, the first time he saw cowboys herding and lassoing cattle, he knew he wanted to be just like them.

The coyotes didn't have rope for him to practice with, so Bill used a rattlesnake. He learned how to lasso real fast! Soon enough, he was the most skilled cowboy in all of Texas. No bucking bronco could throw him—until the day he met that fierce tornado.

By that time, Bill was all grown up and on his own. He had just put his horse, Widow Maker, in her stall. When he stepped outside the barn and bent down to clean some mud off his boots, he felt a tap on his shoulder. He swung around and saw a swirling, roaring-mad tornado staring at him. This was one angry twister!

What had Bill done to make that twister so out of sorts? He didn't know, and chances are, he hadn't done a thing. Tornadoes just like to pick a fight with anyone or anything that gets in their way.

"OK," Bill said, "if that twister wants a fight, I'll certainly give it a fight!"

Pecos Bill stared back at the twister and grabbed his lasso from his belt. He twirled it above his head, starting out slowly. Then he spun the rope faster and faster.

Next Bill tossed his lasso around the twister's waist. He pulled the twister closer and jumped on its back.

Well, the twister did not like this one little bit. It kicked and bucked like a horse, swirling faster and faster. It dragged Bill for hundreds of miles, but Bill held on tight.

The twister was so mad, it started a furious rainstorm. The rain and rushing water made a huge, long hole in the ground. That hole became 277 miles long, 18 miles wide, and 1 mile deep!

Finally, Bill lost his hold and fell off the twister. His body bounced on the ground and landed with a great big thud. His crash landing left another deep hole in the earth—what we now call Death Valley in California.

Now Bill was *really* mad. He twirled his rope and caught the twister by its toes. He kept twisting the rope as tight as he could and held on until that twister was just a tiny cloud in the sky.

Then Bill whistled three times, and Widow Maker came galloping up to him. Pecos Bill hopped on his horse and rode back to look down at that great big canyon the tornado had made—the one we call the Grand Canyon!

18. Based on the details in this story, Pecos Bill can BEST be described as

A. angry.

B. mean.

C. fearless.

D. curious.

19. Which detail from the story is one that shows that Pecos Bill is a larger-than-life character?

A. He hunts at night.

B. He uses a rattlesnake to learn how to lasso.

C. He is the most skilled cowboy in Texas.

D. He survives a tornado.

20. Why does Pecos Bill lasso and ride the twister?

A. because he wants to create the Grand Canyon

B. because he thinks the twister is challenging him

C. because he likes showing off

D. because he needs to get to California

21. What is the purpose of this story?

A. to give an entertaining explanation of how the Grand Canyon was formed

B. to explain why Pecos Bill is the bravest cowboy

C. to tell an entertaining story about life as a cowboy

D. to explain what happens when one is raised by coyotes

22. Explain one reason that the setting in the west is important to the story of Pecos Bill.

_____

_____

_____

_____

_____

Use "Evangeline's Laughter" and "Pecos Bill" to answer questions 23–24.

23. Compare and contrast the use of exaggeration in the two stories. What makes each of them a tall tale?

_____

_____

_____

_____

_____

24. Compare and contrast the characters of Evangeline and Pecos Bill. How do they use their talents?

_____

_____

_____

_____

Part 2: Language Arts

This passage contains mistakes. Read the passage and answer the questions that follow.

The Vet Visit

(1) Ginger barks at me. (2) Then she barks at my mom. (3) She seems to be saying, "Who are these animals? (4) Where are we, and why are we in this strange place?"

(5) I want to tell Ginger that we're here at the vet because she has been limping, and we don't know why. (6) She's even held up her leg and tried to walk on three legs. (7) We want Dr. Ramirez to check out the leg.

(8) Mother and I look around the waiting room, there are all kinds of animals here. (9) I see a sleeping cat in a cage. (10) A lizard <u>lays</u> quietly in a box in a boy's lap. (11) The funniest animal here is the duck standing beside a woman. (12) I am surprised to see that it is wearing a red leash and collar!

(13) Dr. Ramirez leads us into the examination room. (14) Ginger barks in excitement, and Dr. Ramirez smiles. (15) She says, "What a nice bark you have!"

(16) Mother frowns, but I find the doctor's remark amusing. (17) People usually complain about it! (18) Ginger's bark that is deep and loud. (19) The doctor whispers in Ginger's ear, and the dog sits obediently for her. (20) Then, even before Dr. Ramirez can ask to see it, Ginger offers her paw to the doctor.

(21) "Is this the paw that is giving you so much trouble?" she asks Ginger. (22) Ginger is usually shy and won't talk around strangers, so I answer for her. (23) "Yes, that is the one that hurts," I tell the doctor.

(24) Dr. Ramirez turns to me. (25) She asks, "So when did she begin to limp?"

(26) "Yesterday afternoon," I say. (27) Then I add, "I think. (28) I always walk Ginger first thing in the morning. (29) I took her for a thirty-minute walk yesterday morning, too."

(30) Dr. Ramirez has more questions. (31) She asks, "Where do you walk? (32) Do you walk her in the park or on a sidewalk?"

(33) I explain that I walk Ginger on the city's sidewalks for ten blocks and back.

(34) Dr. Ramirez reaches for a small metal tool that looks like a pair of tweezers. (35) She holds Ginger's foot firmly. (36) Then pulls out something small and sharp.

(37) "She stepped on a piece of glass," Dr. Ramirez explains. (38) Ginger wags her tail. (39) She nuzzles the doctor's neck with her nose. (40) "You're welcome!" Dr. Ramirez says.

25. Which of the following is a run-on sentence?

   A. I want to tell Ginger that we're here at the vet because she has been limping, and we don't know why.

   B. Mother and I look around the waiting room, there are all kinds of animals here.

   C. Then, even before Dr. Ramirez can ask to see it, Ginger offers her paw to the doctor.

   D. Ginger is usually shy and won't talk around strangers, so I answer for her.

26. Which of the following is a sentence fragment?

   A. Ginger barks at me.

   B. "I think."

   C. Dr. Ramirez has more questions.

   D. Then pulls out something small and sharp.

27. Which word should replace the underlined word in sentence 10?

   A. lie

   B. lies

   C. laid

   D. lain

28. Why does the conversation between the vet and the narrator MOST LIKELY use informal language?

   A. Informal language makes it harder for the narrator to understand the vet's medical vocabulary.

   B. Informal language makes the young narrator feel at ease about her injured dog.

   C. Informal language allows the vet to use words that the dog will understand.

   D. Informal language isn't used in the conversation because it takes place in a vet's office.

29. Read sentences 34 and 35 from the passage.

> **Dr. Ramirez reaches for a small metal tool that looks like a pair of tweezers. She holds Ginger's foot firmly.**

What is the BEST way to rewrite sentence 35 using a transitional word or phrase?

    A. Next, she holds Ginger's foot firmly.

    B. Therefore, she holds Ginger's foot firmly.

    C. For example, she holds Ginger's foot firmly.

    D. However, she holds Ginger's foot firmly.

30. Read sentences 17 and 18 from the passage.

> **People usually complain about it! Ginger's bark that is deep and loud.**

Which sentence has an error, and what is the error?

_____

_____

_____

Rewrite the sentences to correct the error.

_____

_____

_____

_____

_____

Part 3: Writing

Fictional Narrative Prompt

Going to a place you have never been to before is a way to learn about the different ways people look at and live their lives. It is also a way to learn about yourself. Write a fictional narrative telling about a character or characters who go to a place they have never been to before. The place could be near or far. What does this place look like to your character or characters? Whom do they meet there? What do they do there, and what challenges do they face?

Use the checklist below to help you do your best writing.

Does your fictional narrative

❑ introduce a narrator and/or characters?

❑ set up a situation clearly and have events that follow one another clearly?

❑ use transitional words and phrases to help readers follow the sequence of events?

❑ use details and/or dialogue to show the setting?

❑ use vivid and exact words, phrases, and details?

❑ use a style and vocabulary that make sense for the audience and purpose?

❑ have an interesting conclusion?

❑ use good spelling, capitalization, and punctuation?

❑ follow the rules for good grammar?

Use the following pages to plan and write your response.

Planning Page

Benchmark Assessment 2

Part 1: Reading Comprehension

Read the passage and answer the questions that follow.

A Mighty Woman

The Statue of Liberty is one of the largest statues ever built. It is more than just a statue, though. It is also a monumental symbol, an object that stands for an idea. The idea that the Statue of Liberty represents makes it one of the most welcome sights in the world.

The Idea

During the American Revolution (1775–1783), American colonists fought for freedom from Britain. The French government sent aid to the Americans, which helped them win the war.

About ninety years after the war began, a Frenchman suggested that a monument should be built to celebrate <u>liberty</u>. It would also celebrate the friendship between France and the United States.

The Sculptor

A few years later, in 1871, a well-known French sculptor, Frédéric-Auguste Bartholdi (fray-day-REEK oh-GOOST bar-TOHL-dee), sailed to the United States. He had two reasons for the trip. One was to urge Americans to support the building of the monument. Another was to find the best place for it to stand.

Bartholdi chose Bedloe's Island, not far from the tip of Manhattan. The island was named after Isaac Bedloe, the man who owned it in the 1600s. At one time Bedloe's Island held a fort that protected New York City against attack by enemy ships.

The Symbol

After Bartholdi returned to France, he began to draw the statue he saw in his mind. He wanted it to be huge. According to his design, liberty would be represented by the proud figure of a woman holding a torch. Bartholdi wanted the torch to work like a lighthouse, guiding ships to a safe harbor and lighting the way to liberty for new arrivals.

Other parts of the statue are also symbolic. The seven spikes on Liberty's crown stand for the light of liberty shining on the seven seas and seven continents. In her left arm, Liberty holds a tablet with the date the Declaration of Independence was signed. At her feet lies a broken chain that represents the escape from unjust rulers. Liberty's face, however, is based on that of a real person. Bartholdi used his own mother as the model.

The Statue

France raised about $400,000 for the statue, while people in the United States raised money for the pedestal. American architect Richard Morris Hunt was chosen to design it.

Bartholdi had hoped to have the entire statue ready by 1876, the hundredth anniversary of the signing of the Declaration of Independence. But this was impossible. Instead, he sent the right hand and the torch to the Centennial Exposition in Philadelphia, where the Declaration had been signed. The hand and the torch were later sent on to New York City, which would be the statue's final home.

The Poem

The statue was finally ready in 1886. The city celebrated with a great parade. President Grover Cleveland was there, as were Bartholdi and other French citizens who had taken part in the project.

Though the statue would always stand for the friendship between the United States and France, it came to stand for other ideas as well. For example, a poem called "The New Colossus" was added to the pedestal in 1903. This poem tells about the millions of people who passed the Statue of Liberty on their way to the immigration station on nearby Ellis Island.

In the poem, the poet Emma Lazarus speaks of "A mighty woman with a torch." She imagines Liberty welcoming newcomers to the United States, saying:

Give me your tired, your poor,
Your huddled masses yearning to breathe free . . .
Send them to me, she cries, as I lift my lamp beside the golden door!

Ellis Island no longer receives immigrants, but all those who passed through are remembered in the Museum of Immigration, which opened there in 1990. And together, Ellis Island and Liberty Island (as it has been called since 1956) form the Statue of Liberty National Monument.

1. The word <u>liberty</u> includes the Latin root *liber*. Based on information in this passage, what can you conclude is the meaning of *liber*?

   A. free

   B. large

   C. statue

   D. library

2. Why does the author say that the Statue of Liberty is one of the most welcome sights in the world?

   A. It is a beautiful work of art.

   B. It represents the idea of freedom.

   C. It is one of the largest statues ever built.

   D. It stands near one of the most exciting cities in the world.

3. What is the main idea of the section "The Sculptor"?

   A. Frédéric-Auguste Bartholdi made the Statue of Liberty.

   B. Frédéric-Auguste Bartholdi was a famous French sculptor.

   C. Frédéric-Auguste Bartholdi went to America to begin his monument-building project.

   D. Frédéric-Auguste Bartholdi chose a site near Manhattan for the Statue of Liberty.

4. Why did Frédéric-Auguste Bartholdi send the right hand and torch of the Statue of Liberty to the 1876 Centennial Exposition in Philadelphia?

   A. The rest of the statue was not yet finished.

   B. He wanted to gain more support for his project from Americans.

   C. New York City was not yet ready to display the statue.

   D. The hand represented the signing of the Declaration of Independence.

5. Which of the following questions is answered in this passage?

   A. How many people visit the Statue of Liberty each year?

   B. What other sculptures did Frédéric-Auguste Bartholdi make?

   C. Where does the Statue of Liberty stand?

   D. How much did Americans raise to pay for the statue's pedestal?

6. Based on information in the passage, give two reasons why Frédéric-Auguste Bartholdi wanted to give a monumental statue to the United States.

   _____

   _____

   _____

   _____

Read the story and answer the questions that follow.

Just Waiting for You

"Coreena?"

Coreena heard Mrs. Enfield calling her, even over the sound of the TV, but she didn't answer.

A moment later she heard her name again, this time spoken softly and right next to her ear. That made her jump.

"What?" she snapped. Automatically, she turned the sound off with the remote. At every foster home where she had stayed so far, someone was always telling her to turn down the volume or to turn off the TV, or even angrily lecturing about her watching it so much.

"Hi," said Mrs. Enfield. She smiled as she said it.

"Hi," answered Coreena, carelessly. She turned back to stare at the jumpy movements of the silent cartoon characters on TV. Two short men in animal skins were climbing onto the back of a friendly dinosaur.

"There's something I want to show you on the computer." Mrs. Enfield moved across the room without looking back. She apparently assumed Coreena would follow. Coreena did, though she held back just long enough to make it clear that she did not want to.

She joined her new foster mother at the computer. Mrs. Enfield had another chair beside her own, but Coreena ignored it. She was not planning on staying.

"What do you think?" Mrs. Enfield asked, pointing at the screen. "I thought you'd like to see a real dinosaur."

Coreena found herself interested. She couldn't help it. "What is it?" Of course, it was a dinosaur, or it had been. Actually, it was a drawing of a creature that, according to the scale shown beside it, had been huge.

"It's an image of a newly discovered plant-eating dinosaur. They're calling it *Paralititan*, which means 'tidal giant.'"

"Wow!" said Coreena. She studied the picture. Mrs. Enfield scrolled down the screen and zoomed in on the Paralititan's statistics.

Length: 80–100 feet from snout to tail
Weight: up to 70 tons
Age: about 100 million years old
Period: Late Cretaceous
Where found: Egypt

Coreena finally sat down. Mrs. Enfield moved her chair slightly, and Coreena slid closer.

"You said it was newly discovered," Coreena asked, turning to Mrs. Enfield. "How can that be? I thought people had dug up all these old bones already."

"Not at all," answered Mrs. Enfield as she clicked the mouse to bring up a new screen. This one showed a group of smiling young men and women. They were standing by the newly revealed bones of . . .

"The tidal giant!" Coreena yelled excitedly, pointing at the screen.

Mrs. Enfield nodded.

"Wow," Coreena said again. "So there are still dinosaurs nobody's ever seen before, just waiting to be dug up." She made it sound more like a question than a statement.

"There really are. Scientists unearth more every year," Mrs. Enfield said. She waved her hand toward the computer screen as she said *scientists*.

Coreena was quiet a moment. She was thinking. Thinking about maybe being a dinosaur hunter someday. Thinking about sharing the idea with her mother as soon as she was well again.

"Mrs. Enfield?" said Coreena.

"Call me Mrs. E. That's what my kids have always called me." *My kids*, she called them. Coreena knew she'd had only one child who was now a grown woman. Mrs. E. had meant the foster children she had taken care of over the years.

"Mrs. E.," said Coreena, smiling, "do you think there'll be any new ones left to find by the time I'm ready to be a dinosaur hunter?"

"Coreena, I think that somewhere there's a 'new' dinosaur that's been lying there for millions of years just waiting for you to discover it."

7. Which tells what <u>unearth</u> means as it is used in this story?

   A. bury

   B. dig up

   C. study

   D. put together

8. Why is it important to the story that Coreena is living in a foster home?

   A. It explains why she doesn't know Mrs. Enfield very well.

   B. It explains why she watches so much TV.

   C. It explains why she is interested in dinosaurs.

   D. It explains why she is not at school.

9. Why does Mrs. Enfield want to show Coreena the information about the dinosaur on her computer?

   A. Mrs. Enfield is interested in dinosaurs, too.

   B. Mrs. Enfield wants to talk about something Coreena likes.

   C. Mrs. Enfield thinks Coreena needs to learn more about science.

   D. Mrs. Enfield wants Coreena to explain the information about the dinosaur.

10. Which word BEST describes Coreena at the end of the story?

   A. sad

   B. worried

   C. brave

   D. excited

11. Which sentence BEST states the theme of this story?

    A. Computers are better than TV.

    B. Not all dinosaurs have been discovered by scientists yet.

    C. Talking about personal interests is a way to get to know another person.

    D. Interesting facts can be learned on the computer.

12. Write a short summary of the story. How does Coreena change from the beginning to the end of the story?

    _____

    _____

    _____

    _____

    _____

Read the passage and answer the questions that follow.

A Tale of the *Titanic*

Cheers of excitement erupted from the dock as the largest steamship ever built began its first voyage. On April 10, 1912, the *Titanic* left Southampton, England, and headed toward New York City. The giant ship carried 2,224 passengers and crew—and enough lifeboats for only about half of them.

Sinkable? Unthinkable!

The *Titanic* was thought to be unsinkable. The bottom part of the ship, called the hull, was divided into sixteen compartments, or rooms. Each compartment was supposed to be watertight. Even if water did fill as many as four compartments, the ship would still be able to float. No one imagined that even that many compartments could fill with water.

Four days into the ship's first trip, however, the unimaginable actually happened. About four hundred miles south of Newfoundland, the *Titanic* slammed into an iceberg. The crash ripped apart the ship's hull. At least five of the compartments at the front of the ship were damaged, and four of them filled with water. The weight of the water pulled down the front of the ship. Water flowed into more and more compartments, pulling the front of the ship farther under the water. In just a few hours, the ship fell more than two miles to the bottom of the cold North Atlantic sea.

Only 705 people survived. Not only did the ship not carry enough lifeboats, but many lifeboats left the ship only partly full. Also, although another ship, the *Californian,* was only twenty miles away, it never came to help. No one on the *Californian* was on duty to hear the call for help that the *Titanic* was sending by radio. A different ship, *Carpathia,* arrived more than an hour after the *Titanic* sank—soon enough to save some lives, but not everyone.

The tragedy captured the imagination of the public. The *Titanic* had been a glamorous ship, and many of the people who lost their lives were just as glamorous. In the decades since, many stories and films and a musical have been made about the sinking of the *Titanic.* The tragedy resulted in more than just a stream of sad and romantic stories, though. At a meeting in London in 1913, new rules were set to make travel by ship safer. For example, it was required that every ship have enough lifeboats for every person on board. (Believe it or not, the *Titanic* actually had *more* lifeboats on board than it was required to have at the time!)

Fast Forward to 1985

Imagine a video camera gliding along the bottom of the ocean. You peer into the video camera's monitor located aboard your ship, but all it reveals is murky darkness. Then, suddenly, an enormous shape looms up in front of you. It's the wreck of the *Titanic*!

In 1985, Jean-Louis Michel and Robert Ballard discovered the final resting place of the rusty, broken ship. A year later, Ballard and his team returned and used a special submarine to explore the site. Doorknobs and statues, a doll's head, shoes, and silver trays appeared before them. A locked safe, a broken bench—thousands of objects had spilled from the ship as it sunk. The people who had perished on the *Titanic* were gone, but the items they left behind have become treasures of the past, relics of life on board a doomed ship.

13. Read this sentence from the passage.

> **Only 705 people survived.**

How does this sentence compare with the other sentences in paragraph 4 of the passage?

A. It is an effect of the causes described in the paragraph.

B. It is a solution for the problems described in the paragraph.

C. It is a problem that causes other problems suggested in the paragraph.

D. It is a cause of the effects described in the paragraph.

14. Which sentence from the passage BEST supports the idea that the tragedy of the *Titanic* captured the imagination of the public?

A. "A different ship, *Carpathia,* arrived more than an hour after the *Titanic* sank—soon enough to save some lives, but not everyone."

B. "The *Titanic* had been a glamorous ship, and many of the people who lost their lives were just as glamorous."

C. "In the decades since, many stories and films and a musical have been made about the sinking of the *Titanic.*"

D. "At a meeting in London in 1913, new rules were set to make travel by ship safer."

15. What does paragraph 5 MOSTLY tell about?

A. the effects of the sinking of the *Titanic*

B. the causes of the sinking of the *Titanic*

C. the contrasts between rules before and after the *Titanic* sank

D. the contrasts between stories told before and after the *Titanic* sank

16. Read this sentence from the passage.

> **At a meeting in London in 1913, new rules were set to make travel by ship safer.**

What can you conclude from this statement?

A. No one died at sea ever again.

B. The captain of the *Titanic* had broken those rules.

C. The new rules made people feel better about traveling at sea.

D. Ships were no longer in danger of hitting icebergs.

17. What is the section "Fast Forward to 1985" MOSTLY about?

    A. the sinking of the *Titanic*

    B. the discovery of the wreck of the *Titanic*

    C. the objects found on the wreck of the *Titanic*

    D. the methods and tools used to explore the *Titanic*

18. Why was the *Titanic* thought to be unsinkable? Give at least two details from the passage that explain why.

    _____

    _____

    _____

    _____

    _____

Read the passage and answer the questions that follow.

In the Shadow of a Volcano

If you lived in Pompeii almost two thousand years ago, August 24 would have seemed like a typical day. True, the earth shook slightly, and animals were restless. But that had happened before. Smoke rising from the nearby volcano was odd, not frightening. Then suddenly, around noon, Mount Vesuvius roared to life.

A huge column of fiery ash and rock shot from the volcano. "Darkness fell . . . as if the lamp had been put out," a teenage eyewitness wrote. Thousands of people fled the city. Many hid in their houses. Burning ash and cinders rained down. Around midnight, an avalanche of rock, ash, and volcanic gas barreled down the mountainside. By morning, Pompeii was buried.

A Forgotten City

In the following days, some who had escaped returned to dig out their houses. But poisonous gases made it too dangerous. People gave up, and, eventually, no one came back. Pompeii was deserted. Gradually, the ash hardened. Grass grew over the site. And people forgot the city beneath the green fields.

One day in the late 1500s, workers were digging a canal when they unearthed some paintings and slabs of marble. They did not know, however, that they had found the ruins of Pompeii. Many years later, in 1748, Charles III of Naples and Sicily ordered that the site be dug up. He was not interested in having people study the ruins, though. He wanted to take treasures from the site to add to his personal collection.

Although the early work at Pompeii and nearby Herculaneum are thought of as the beginnings of archaeology, much of it was done without care or thought. Also, Charles III was not the only person hoping to take treasures from the site. Looters tore through the area, too. They didn't care what damage they caused.

In 1763, an <u>inscription</u> was found with words that identified the site as Pompeii. But was the city already on its way to ruin again?

Trapped in Time

During the 1800s, archaeologist Giuseppe Fiorelli took charge of the site. Under his direction, work was done more carefully. Many of Pompeii's houses and shops were preserved, and findings were recorded. It was discovered that volcanic ash had buried people alive! Over time, the bodies had decayed. But the shapes of the bodies remained as holes in the hardened ash. So Fiorelli figured out a way to show us the people of Pompeii.

He began by pouring plaster into the holes and letting it harden. Then he chipped away the ash that surrounded each form. The statues that emerged capture terrible moments from long ago. A family huddles together in their cellar. A man lies at the city gate, holding his pair of shoes. A dog struggles to pull free from its chain.

Pompeii: Then and Now

Over the years, archaeologists have discovered rakes, milk pitchers, and even bread preserved in the ashes. They've also found graffiti on the walls. One urges people to vote for a man because he makes good bread. Another is a love note to a girl named Victoria.

If you visited Pompeii today, you could walk its narrow, cobblestoned streets. You might tour a villa where wealthy people once lived. You could sit in the amphitheater and imagine a crowd cheering the gladiators. And if you looked across the countryside, you'd see Mount Vesuvius, looming over the city.

19. Read this sentence from the passage.

> **In 1763, an <u>inscription</u> was found with words that identified the site as Pompeii.**

The word <u>inscription</u> is based on the Latin root *scribere.* Based on information in this sentence, what can you conclude is the meaning of *scribere*?

A. to find

B. to write

C. to tell

D. to keep

20. Read this statement from the passage.

> **"Darkness fell . . . as if the lamp had been put out."**

How does the viewpoint in this statement differ from the viewpoint in the rest of the passage?

A. It shows how someone who was really there saw the eruption.

B. It gives a fact about the day Pompeii was buried.

C. It explains what happened when Mount Vesuvius erupted.

D. It tells why people ran from Pompeii.

21. What can you conclude from paragraph 5 of the passage?

A. None of the treasures of Pompeii are left at the site.

B. Looting is no longer a problem at the site of Pompeii.

C. Looters have done more damage to Pompeii than Mount Vesuvius did.

D. Many objects from Pompeii that would have been good to study have been stolen.

22. Why was the work of Giuseppe Fiorelli important?

A. He made it possible to learn about Pompeii's past.

B. He discovered that people died when Mount Vesuvius erupted.

C. He recovered many of the objects that were taken from Pompeii.

D. He found that the site uncovered in the late 1500s was actually Pompeii.

23. Which of the following questions is answered in this passage?

    A. Why did Mount Vesuvius erupt?

    B. What poisonous gases remained after Mount Vesuvius erupted?

    C. Why did Charles III want the site of Pompeii to be dug up?

    D. What treasures did looters steal from the site of Pompeii?

24. How has the work of archaeologists shown how the people of Pompeii lived? Give at least two details from the passage.

_____

_____

_____

_____

_____

Part 2: Language Arts

This passage contains mistakes. Read the passage and answer the questions that follow.

Taking Flight

(1) In 1900, travel was more difficult than it is now. (2) It was harder to get around. (3) People often walked many miles. (4) For long-distance travel, they rode trains or horses. (5) One thing people couldn't do was fly. (6) There were no airplanes. (7) In fact, to most people, the very idea of flying seemed impossible. (8) Humans dreamed of being able to fly like birds, but few thought it would ever happen.

(9) One person who dreamed about flying was Jules Verne, a popular writer. (10) His books described people taking imaginery trips in airplanes and spaceships. (11) Most readers thought his ideas could never become real, they thought he was just a dreamer. (12) But Verne's ideas were based on new discoveries in science. (13) In fact, many of the things he described have since come true.

(14) Many inventers of the early 1900s were trying to build airplanes or flying machines. (15) Some of their experiments came to an unlucky end when their planes crashed. (16) But they made important discoveries even <u>thorough</u> these failures. (17) They learned about what holds an airplane up in the air. (18) They learned what kind of controls an airplane needed to have so it wouldn't crash. (19) They wrote about what they learned.

(20) Wilbur and Orville Wright studied these reports and learned about the new discoveries. (21) Then built a new kind of airplane. (22) In 1903, their plane flew 120 feet in North Carolina. (23) It was the first successful airplane flight in history. (24) The exciting age of air travel had begun.

(25) Air travel grew unbelievably fast. (26) Airplanes could soon fly a hundred miles without stopping. (27) Planes started carrying passengers. (28) In 1927, Charles Lindbergh flew alone to France. (29) Lindbergh wrote a book recalling his flight. (30) He said flying made him feel like he "owned the world." (31) In the 1950s, jet airplanes became common. (32) They carried hundreds of passengers. (33) By the 1960s, people were exploring space. (34) Nations raced to be first on the moon. (35) In 1969, Americans landed on the moon. (36) People had gone from horseback to spaceships in less than seventy years

25. Which of the following is a sentence fragment?

   A. There were no airplanes.

   B. They wrote about what they learned.

   C. Then built a new kind of airplane.

   D. Air travel grew unbelievably fast.

26. Which word should replace the underlined word in sentence 16?

   A. thru

   B. threw

   C. though

   D. through

27. Read sentence 28 from the passage.

> **In 1927, Charles Lindbergh flew alone to France.**

Which is the BEST prepositional phrase to add to the end of sentence 28?

   A. in his airplane

   B. from New York

   C. up in the sky

   D. without help

28. Read sentence 36 from the passage.

> **People had gone from horseback to spaceships in less than seventy years**

Which is the BEST way to punctuate sentence 36?

   A. People had gone from horseback to spaceships, in less than 70 years.

   B. People had gone from horseback to spaceships in less than 70 years!

   C. People had gone from horseback to spaceships in less than 70 years?

   D. People had gone from horseback to spaceships in less than 70 years. . . .

29. Which word from the passage is spelled correctly?

    A. impossable

    B. imaginery

    C. inventers

    D. passengers

30. Read sentence 11 from the passage.

> **Most readers thought his ideas could never become real, they thought he was just a dreamer.**

What is the error in this sentence?

_____

_____

_____

Rewrite the sentence to correct the error.

_____

_____

_____

_____

_____

Part 3: Writing

Personal Narrative Prompt

Making a new friend is exciting! Write a personal narrative telling about a time you made a new friend. How did you meet your friend? What did you notice about your friend at first? How did you become friends? What do you and your friend do together, and what do you know about your friend now that you didn't know at first?

Use the checklist below to help you do your best writing.

Does your personal narrative

❑ introduce characters?

❑ set up a situation clearly and have events that follow one another clearly?

❑ use transitional words and phrases to help readers follow the sequence of events?

❑ use details to show the characters?

❑ use vivid and exact words, phrases, and details?

❑ use a style and vocabulary that make sense for the audience and purpose?

❑ have an interesting conclusion?

❑ use good spelling, capitalization, and punctuation?

❑ follow the rules for good grammar?

Use the following pages to plan and write your response.

Planning Page

Benchmark Assessment 3

Part 1: Reading Comprehension

Read the play and answer the questions that follow.

A New Beginning

CAST OF CHARACTERS

PAPA
MAMA
MARY
ROSA
PRESIDENT ROOSEVELT (*heard over the radio*)

Scene One

(*Papa, Mama, and Mary are traveling in a car covered in dirt.*)

PAPA: (*sighs*) It's sad we're leaving the farm, but we had to get away from those dust storms.

MARY: Can you see the road, Papa?

PAPA: Not very well, Mary. Those dark, dust clouds have blocked the sun. It's like driving in a black fog.

MARY: Will we go back to Oklahoma when the dust storms are gone?

MAMA: I don't know, Mary. We'll find a new place to live in California. We could be so happy there that we may never want to return.

MARY: Oh, but Mama, I already miss the farm. I can't imagine living anywhere else. . .

Scene Two

(*Mary has dropped her books in the schoolyard. Rosa is helping her collect them.*)

MARY: Thanks so much for helping me. My name is Mary.

ROSA: I'm Rosa. Are you new here?

MARY: We just moved here from Oklahoma.

ROSA: I moved here, too! But that was two years ago. Why did you move?

MARY: Last year there was a <u>drought</u>. The rain never came. Then there were dust storms, and our farm was ruined. At night, I slept with a towel over my face to keep the dust off! We had to leave everything behind. It was scary.

ROSA: We're farmers, too. We left Mexico to come here. At first, I was sad. Now I'm happier. I like my new school and my new friends.

MARY: I wish I was still in Oklahoma. I miss our old farm. Everything here is so different, and I don't know anyone.

ROSA: I know what you mean. It was strange at first. But then I made new friends. And I went to the ocean and saw the mountains on the coast.

MARY: Oh! The ocean! I've never seen it. And mountains! Oklahoma is so flat.

ROSA: There is a lot to see in California.

MARY: Maybe it won't be so bad here.

ROSA: Just wait until you get settled. You'll see.

MARY: Thanks, Rosa. You really helped me feel better.

Scene Three

(Mary's family and Rosa are gathered around a radio in Mary's new home.)

PRESIDENT ROOSEVELT: (*over the radio*) The test of our progress is not whether we add more to the abundance of those who have much; it is whether we <u>provide</u> enough for those who have too little.

MARY: I don't understand what the president means. What is *abundance*?

MAMA: Remember the days when we had a big harvest? We enjoyed abundance then. We had everything we needed and more. So the president is saying that we are a better country if we help people who do not have everything they need, like our neighbors who are still in Oklahoma.

ROSA: I'm sure glad you left when you did.

PAPA: I agree, Rosa. I was lucky to find work here, and Mary seems happy in her new school. Many of our friends back in Oklahoma aren't so lucky. They lost a lot. They didn't leave in time, like we did. Where they live is now called the Dust Bowl.

MAMA: You know, President Roosevelt is going to help our friends. Soon, the land will get better. Then people will be back at work on their farms.

MARY: (*interrupting excitedly*) Yes! Then we can go visit, but not to stay. There's so much to see here!

ROSA: I can't wait to go with you to the ocean!

1. How do you know that "A New Beginning" is a play rather than a story written in prose?

   A. It is mostly dialogue.

   B. It includes several characters.

   C. It is mostly description.

   D. It tells about the past.

2. Which word means the OPPOSITE of drought?

   A. flood

   B. harvest

   C. farm

   D. dust

3. Which word means the same as provide as it is used in this play?

   A. improve

   B. subtract

   C. hunger

   D. give

4. What is one difference between California and Oklahoma that is important to the play?

   A. Oklahoma has farms, but California does not.

   B. Oklahoma has a drought, but California has dust storms.

   C. California is near the ocean, but Oklahoma is far away.

   D. California has schools, but Oklahoma does not.

5. Read these sentences from the play.

"Then we can go visit, but not to stay. There's so much to see here!"

What can you conclude from these sentences?

A. Mary enjoys living in California.

B. Mary likes to move to new places.

C. Mary does not care about Oklahoma anymore.

D. Mary wants to show her neighbors how lucky she is.

6. Write a short summary of the play. How do Mary's feelings change from the beginning to the end of the play?

_____

_____

_____

_____

Read the passage and answer the questions that follow.

Miracle on Ice

When the U.S. hockey team faced the Soviet Union in the 1980 Olympics, it was almost certain that the game would end with a victory for the Soviets. It was so certain, in fact, that the television network ABC didn't even bother to show the game live. After all, the Soviet hockey team won *everything*. The players practiced together eleven months of the year. During that time, they did nothing but eat, sleep, and breathe hockey.

Plus, just three weeks earlier, the U.S. hockey team had faced the Soviet Union in a game at Madison Square Garden. The result? A 10–3 win for the Soviets.

However, in the weeks since that crushing loss, the U.S. team had had two important victories. In their first game in the Olympic tournament, they tied Sweden 2–2. In fact, the United States tied the game with only twenty-seven seconds left—and with their goalie on the bench! Although they did not win the game, this tie was a victory for the Americans. Since 1960 they had lost every other game they had played against Sweden.

The U.S. team took the energy from this game into their next game, against Czechoslovakia. The Czechs were expected to win the silver medal. But they lost badly to the United States, 7–3. All seven U.S. goals were scored by a different player.

Nevertheless, the Americans went into the game against the Soviet Union as underdogs. U.S. coach Herb Brooks wanted to make sure that his team didn't feel like underdogs. For example, he told them that the Soviet Union's greatest player, Boris Mikhailov, looked like the comedian Stan Laurel. They could beat a comedian on ice, couldn't they?

The first big moment of the game came at the end of the first period. The score was 2–1 with the Soviets in the lead. U.S. player Dave Christian took a shot at the goal. The Soviet goalkeeper, Vladislav Tretiak, saved the shot, but the puck bounced off his pads. The puck went straight toward U.S. player Mark Johnson, who took another shot and scored a goal. The game was tied with just one second left in the first period. The Soviet coach, Viktor Tikhonov, was so upset that he removed Tretiak from the game. Years later, Tikhonov said that he never made a bigger mistake.

Meanwhile, the American goalie, Jim Craig, was doing an excellent job. The Soviets were getting many shots at the goal, but after the first period, only one more shot made it past Craig. Soviet player Alexander Maltsev scored that goal in the second period. No one else scored in the second period, so at the beginning of the third period, the score was 3–2, with the Soviet Union winning.

The key goals for the United States came quickly in the middle of the third period. At about eight and a half minutes into the period, Johnson scored for a second time to tie the game. Just a minute and a half later, Mike Eruzione scored again. For the first time, the United States had the lead. For the ten minutes left in the game, they did not let go of the lead. Craig would not let the Soviets score. Toward the end of the game, the <u>spectators</u> went wild. They counted down the last ten seconds of the game—until, to everyone's surprise, the United States won!

Two days later, the United States beat Finland 4–2 to win the gold medal. But that game is not the one that everyone remembers from the 1980 Olympics. The most memorable game was the miracle on ice, in which the United States beat the best team in the world.

Ice Hockey Basics

The following are some of the basic rules in hockey:

- Each team has six players, including a goalie.

- The game is played with a puck, which is a rubber disk that slides on ice. Players move the puck with hockey sticks.

- The object of the game is to get the puck into the other team's goal. The goalie's job is to protect the goal.

- A team scores one point for each goal.

- The game lasts sixty minutes, which are divided into three twenty-minute periods. The team with the most points at the end of the game wins.

7. Which detail from the passage BEST supports the idea that the Americans were likely to lose to the Soviets?

    A. They had not won a game against the Swedes since 1960.

    B. Czechoslovakia was expected to win the silver medal.

    C. The Soviet's greatest player looked like a comedian.

    D. The Americans had recently lost badly to the same Soviet team.

8. Read this sentence from the passage.

    Years later, Tikhonov said that he never made a bigger mistake.

    What can you conclude from this sentence?

    A. Tikhonov believed that he should not have gotten upset.

    B. Tikhonov believed that the Soviets would have won if he'd kept Tretiak in the game.

    C. Tikhonov believed that Tretiak lost the game for the Soviet Union.

    D. Tikhonov believed that he should have tried to play in the game himself.

9. Read this sentence from the passage.

    Meanwhile, the American goalie, Jim Craig, was doing an excellent job.

    In this sentence, Jim Craig is contrasted with

    A. Vladislav Tretiak.

    B. Mark Johnson.

    C. Viktor Tikhonov.

    D. Alexander Maltsev.

10. The Latin root *spectare* means "to look." Which tells what spectators means as it is used in this passage?

    A. those who are excited

    B. those who yell

    C. those who play

    D. those who watch

11. Which of the following questions is answered in this passage?

    A. What other games did the Soviet team play in the 1980 Olympics?

    B. Who was the goalie for the Soviets after Tretiak was removed from the game?

    C. Who scored the winning goal for the Americans?

    D. How many other Olympic gold medals has the U.S. hockey team won?

12. What is one reason why the U.S. hockey team could feel confident in their game against the Soviets? What is one reason why the U.S. hockey team felt like underdogs?

    _____

    _____

    _____

    _____

    _____

Read the poem and answer the questions that follow.

The Ballad of Sally

Sally was a brave gal:
There was no one she wouldn't face;
Nor was there any creature
That Sally wouldn't race.

5   Sally was in the garden
Singing to the peas
When her little kids came yelling,
"Mama, come help us, please!
The dog is trapped inside the barn
10   With a swarm of angry bees!"

Sally grabbed some clover.
She started chewing fast.
She faced the buzzers eye-to-eye
And breathed out with a blast.

15   Sally's breath was oh-so-strong
From the clover. It was sweet.
Whoosh! Into a hollow log
The bees' little wings did beat.

Then Sally put her hand inside.
20   She felt a sticky goo.
"I've taught them to make honey.
Now, kids, here's a treat!
We have plenty of honey to eat!"

13. Read line 2 from the poem.

> **There was no one she
> wouldn't face**

Which line from the poem ends with a word that rhymes with *face*?

A. line 1

B. line 3

C. line 4

D. line 5

14. Which syllables are stressed in line 3?

A. <u>Nor</u> was there any <u>creature</u>

B. Nor <u>was</u> there <u>any</u> <u>creature</u>

C. <u>Nor</u> was <u>there</u> any <u>creature</u>

D. <u>Nor</u> <u>was</u> there any <u>creature</u>

15. Which is the BEST summary of this poem?

A. Sally is brave and will take on any challenge.

B. Sally's dog is trapped inside a barn filled with angry bees.

C. Sally saves her dog by using clover to calm a swarm of bees.

D. Sally finds honey that some bees have made.

16. How did the bees make honey?

A. by biting the dog

B. by eating wood inside the log

C. by flying out of the barn so quickly

D. by using the clover on Sally's breath

17. Based on events in this poem, what can you conclude about Sally?

    A. She is clever as well as brave.

    B. She is not really brave.

    C. She does not like bees.

    D. She has bad breath.

18. How do you know that "The Ballad of Sally" is a poem? Write two ways that it is different from a story in prose.

    _____

    _____

    _____

    _____

    _____

Read the poem and answer the questions that follow.

Cloud Forest

The wonders of the cloud forest are a most dazzling sight.
The <u>titanic</u> mountains fade into the fog.
Patches of darkness let through bursts of sunlight.
Water spills into pools in a valley of green

5   The deep silence is broken only by drips.
Water falls from leaves as the lake waves hello.
I touch a tree with my small fingertips,
And breathe in the fresh air, the weather so cool.

Then a rush of a waterfall gets me up from my knees.
10   I listen for a second before following the sound.
It reminds me of the ocean as I walk through the trees.
There are flowers in the forest. There's life all around.

I see flashes of color—so many birds!
But they'll all go away if we don't save these woods.
15   The songs of these creatures will no longer be heard;
If we keep cutting down trees, they'll be gone for good.

I turn a corner, and finally I see
The clearest waterfall racing right down a mountain.
It looks like a dream just waiting for me.
20   I walk right up and put my hand in this fountain.

With the mountains behind us and the clouds above,
We hike through this forest we'll never forget.
The animals need us to act out of love.
We must save their home. It's the only one they will get.

19. Which lines in the first stanza end with rhyming words?

    A. lines 1 and 2

    B. lines 1 and 3

    C. lines 1 and 4

    D. lines 2 and 4

20. Which word means the same as <u>titanic</u> as it is used in this poem?

    A. huge

    B. rocky

    C. boat

    D. cold

21. In the poem, the speaker uses the words "flashes of color" as a metaphor for

    A. the forest.

    B. flowers.

    C. birds.

    D. birdsong.

22. Which sentence BEST states the theme of the poem?

    A. The forest is beautiful.

    B. People are destroying the forest.

    C. The beauty of the forest should be saved.

    D. Hiking through the forest cannot be forgotten.

23. Read this stanza from the poem.

> **I turn a corner, and finally I see**
> **The clearest waterfall racing right down a mountain.**
> **It looks like a dream just waiting for me.**
> **I walk right up and put my hand in this fountain.**

In this stanza, the speaker uses a simile to compare the waterfall to a

A. race.

B. mountain.

C. dream.

D. friend.

24. How is the way the speaker describes the setting important to the theme of this poem?

_____

_____

_____

_____

_____

Part 2: Language Arts

This passage contains mistakes. Read the passage and answer the questions that follow.

Fox River

(1) Jon Larsen felt happy. (2) The settlement at Fox River, Illinois, was getting better every day. (3) Jon's family and sevral others had come here from Norway five years ago. (4) They worked hard to build Fox River into a strong colony.

(5) "This land is good. (6) There is plenty of food for all families," Jon had written to his parents. (7) His letters convinced his parents, Ole and Ingrid, to come.

(8) Jon was overjoyed when his parents arrived. (9) "Mother! Father!" he said. (10) "I am so happy to see you! (11) Welcome to our wonderful colony at Fox River."

(12) "You settlers have done such exellent work! (13) How have you done so much in five years?" Ole asked his son.

(14) "We do so much because we help each other out," said Jon. (15) "For example, we have a great carpenter named Lars. (16) He showed us how to cut down trees safely. (17) Then he helped us build our houses and barns. (18) Which are very warm and dry. (19) Whenever a new family comes, we immedeately build their house and barn. (20) We want them to feel welcome.

(21) "Erik helps them start their farms. (22) He is a very cheerful fellow and makes the newcomers feel happy. (23) His wife Freya is very kind, too. (24) She finds room for them in their home and feeds them. (25) Erik and Freya never expect to get paid for their help.

(26) "We have a doctor named Gudmund. (27) He is an educated man. (28) He mends our cuts and broken bones. (29) Last year when cholera struck the colony, he saved many lives. (30) We would not have been able to survive without his help."

(31) Then Jon pointed to a small building. (32) He explained to his parents that it was the schoolhouse. (33) "Mrs. Hanson teaches our children to read, write, and do math," he said. (34) "All of the students study hard. (35) Our son Nils wants to be a writer. (36) He has already written exciting stories about our life here in Fox River."

(37) "We're so glad we moved to Fox River with you," Ingrid said. (38) "We were scared to come. (39) But we knew it was the right thing to do. (40) You have all made such a good life here. (41) I know we will do that, too."

(42) "Yes, we are so proud of you, son," Ole said.

(43) "Come, then. Let's find Lars," said Jon, happily. (44) "We need to build you a house!"

25. Which of the following is a sentence fragment?

    A. Welcome to our wonderful colony at Fox River.

    B. Which are very warm and dry.

    C. Erik helps them start their farms.

    D. He is an educated man.

26. Read sentence 5 from the passage.

    This land is good.

Which is the BEST prepositional phrase to add to the end of sentence 5?

    A. with farming

    B. for farming

    C. to farming

    D. on farming

27. Suppose John Larsen was writing a letter to a land management agency asking about buying land instead of a letter to his parents urging them to move to Fox River. How might his language differ?

    A. Larsen would use formal language because of the subject and the recipient.

    B. Larsen would use formal language because it is easier to understand.

    C. Larsen would use informal language because of the subject and the recipient.

    D. Larsen would use informal language because it is easier to understand.

28. Read sentence 34 from the passage.

    All of the students study hard.

What is a way to write this sentence to show that the students began to study hard in the past and continue to study hard now?

    A. All of the students studying hard.

    B. All of the students have studied hard.

    C. All of the students have been studying hard.

    D. All of the students will study hard.

29. Which word from the passage is spelled correctly?

    A. sevral

    B. exellent

    C. immedeately

    D. exciting

30. Read sentence 14 from the passage.

    "We do so much because we help each other out," said Jon.

Rewrite the sentence by adding the helping verb *can*.

_____

_____

_____

Part 3: Writing

Read the story and respond to the prompt that follows.

Out of the Light, Into the Night
adapted from a Native American (Anishinabe) story

You who are afraid of the night, come closer. Sit as near to the bright fire as you dare. Now look to your right and to your left. Your friends are near you, are they not? So you can see that you have nothing to fear. It is important that you are not afraid here in the night. And it is important that you understand this: The night creature I will tell you about is not to be feared, either.

Just as you rise with the Sun and sleep when he sleeps, so do many of the creatures of the forest. That's why it was so strange one morning long ago when the Sun's light did not shine. Owl did not mind, for she hunts at night. But those who flee her claws were worn out.

"Where is the Sun?" asked the field mouse and a little green frog. Soon, even the birds and the animals that hunt by day understood that somehow the Sun was missing.

It was a small, brown squirrel that found the missing Sun. High up in the branches above the forest floor, the squirrel could see for miles. At first it saw only darkness. But finally, far off to the east, it saw a glow.

Hopping from tree to tree, the squirrel climbed closer and closer to the light. When it was very close, it saw that the glow came from the Sun. But the Sun was weak and pale. The Sun had become caught in the branches of a very high tree. The harder he tried to free himself, the more tangled he got.

The Sun begged the squirrel, "Help me!"

The squirrel thought about what it could do to help. Then, using its sharp teeth, it began to bite at one of the branches that held the Sun. Soon the squirrel had bitten clear through the branch.

The Sun sighed. "That's good. Keep working."

The squirrel moved from branch to branch, gnawing away. It was warm work, though. Each time the Sun broke free from another branch, it grew stronger and hotter.

"I must stop," said the squirrel. "I'm burning!"

It was true. The heat from the Sun had turned the little brown squirrel's fur to the color of ashes.

"Don't stop!" said the Sun. "I'm almost free."

Again the squirrel listened to the Sun's plea. Again it freed another branch. And again the Sun grew still hotter.

"I'm burning from the heat," said the squirrel. "Even my tail has burned away!"

"Just a little more," pleaded the Sun. "A little more!"

Once more the squirrel went to work. It was nearly blind from the brightness of the Sun, but it sensed when the Sun was finally freed from the branches. Soon the Sun was riding high in the sky, where it was supposed to be.

Even from that height, though, the Sun could see the poor squirrel. Gone were its bushy tail and the brown fur that had covered its body. His eyes were closed against the brightness of the Sun.

"Poor thing," said the Sun. "You helped me, and now I will help you. What one thing have you wanted to do all your life?"

"Fly," was the squirrel's simple answer.

"Then so you shall. But you will fly only at night, when you won't have to face my bright light."

With that, the creature that had once been a squirrel spread its new wings and began to fly. And so it does every night when the Sun goes down in the west. For that is how the first bat came to be.

Response to Literature Prompt

> Describe the squirrel in "Out of the Light, Into the Night." What do you learn about the squirrel from its thoughts? What do you learn from its words? What do you learn from its actions? Why does the Sun reward the squirrel at the end of the story?
>
> Use the checklist below to help you do your best writing.

Does your response to literature

❑ introduce a topic?

❑ group related ideas in an organized structure?

❑ include details from the text to support your opinion and reasons?

❑ use transitional words and phrases to help readers follow your opinion and reasons?

❑ use a style and vocabulary that make sense for the audience and purpose?

❑ have a conclusion that sums up the topic?

❑ use good spelling, capitalization, and punctuation?

❑ follow the rules for good grammar?

Use the following pages to plan and write your response.

Planning Page

Benchmark Assessment 4

Part 1: Reading Comprehension

Read the passage and answer the questions that follow.

The Truth about Bats

You have probably heard the phrase "blind as a bat" dozens of times. The phrase is so familiar that few people question it. But is it true? Are bats really blind? Or has this saying simply been repeated so many times that everyone thinks it is true? As a matter of fact, it is not true. Bats actually have excellent eyesight. You may wonder, then, how many other common beliefs about bats are actually true.

Bats are often thought to be frightening and even dangerous. For example, it has been said that you should cover your head around bats, because they can get tangled in your hair. Some people even believe that bats are like vampires and live on the blood of humans. These ideas are silly. Unless you happen to be wearing a nest of insects as a hat, bats are certainly not interested in your hair. And although there is a kind of bat called a vampire bat, it is unlikely to be any danger to you. For one thing, it feeds on the blood of other animals, such as cattle. It rarely bites human beings. And anyway, vampire bats are not found in North America.

However, a wide variety of bats do live in North America—and indeed, throughout the world. In fact, bats can be found just about everywhere on the globe, except for the cold polar regions. There are nearly one thousand different species of bats. They come in many colors and sizes. There are brown bats and black bats, as you probably imagine. But other bats have bright colors and markings—even yellow, red, and silver. And, whereas the smallest bat is about the size of a bumblebee, the largest has a wingspan of six feet (1.8 meters). Most North American bats are fairly small, with a wingspan of about twelve inches (thirty centimeters).

Bats are actually helpful to humans. Some bats eat fruit or other things, but most eat insects. Many of the insects that bats eat are harmful—and bats can eat *a lot* of insects. For example, a brown bat can eat a thousand mosquitoes in just one hour! Why do bats have such a bad reputation, then? It may be because most are nocturnal. In other words, they sleep during the day and are active at night. They are nocturnal for good reasons. As small mammals, they are safer from large predators at night. Also, at night they don't have to compete with birds (many of which eat insects, too) for their food.

Like birds, of course, bats can fly. They are the only mammals that can fly. The mammals called flying squirrels and flying lemurs can glide, but they do not actually fly. Bats, on the other hand, use their wings to move themselves through the air, as birds do. Their wings are not like the wings of a bird, though. Their wings are made of a double layer of skin stretched over the bones of their arms and long, slender fingers. Bats fly more easily than they walk. But their feet have extremely strong claws. These claws can support the entire weight of a bat.

Do bats really sleep upside down? This common image of bats is based in fact. It is their strong claws that make their upside-down sleep possible. They are actually more comfortable hanging upside down than they are upright!

1. What is this passage MOSTLY about?

   A. familiar sayings about bats

   B. silly ideas people have about bats

   C. the wide variety of bats in the world

   D. the facts among common ideas about bats

2. What can you infer from paragraph 1?

   A. Ideas that are repeated often are often believed.

   B. Familiar sayings are usually based on fact.

   C. Something that most people believe is probably not true.

   D. It is impossible to know what is true and what is false.

3. According to the passage, why might people think bats are frightening?

   A. Bats sometimes bite human beings.

   B. Some bats are quite large.

   C. Most bats are nocturnal.

   D. Bats eat insects.

4. According to the passage, which belief about bats is actually true?

   A. Bats cannot see.

   B. Bats get tangled in human hair.

   C. Bats are only brown or black.

   D. Bats sleep upside down.

5. Which text structure is used in paragraph 5 of the passage?

   A. cause and effect

   B. problem and solution

   C. compare and contrast

   D. chronological order

6. For what reasons is it helpful for bats to be active at night rather than during the day? Give two reasons from the passage.

   _____

   _____

   _____

   _____

   _____

Read the play and answer the questions that follow.

Problem in the Palace

CAST OF CHARACTERS

KING   DASHING DEREK
QUEEN   PALACE LADIES
PRINCESS GORGONZOLA   SERVANTS
DOCTOR SNOZZARELLO   PAGE

Scene One

A palace hallway. The walls of the hallway are lined with tall mirrors. The king and queen give directions to a half dozen servants. The shrieks and sobs of a young woman can be heard off stage.

KING: Cover all the mirrors in the palace! And quickly! (*The servants rush to cover the mirrors with curtains.*)

QUEEN: And hide all the handheld mirrors! (*Two servants curtsy and scurry off stage.*) Now, everybody, smile. Here comes the princess!

The servants smile and curtsy as Princess Gorgonzola walks on stage, still sobbing. She is a lovely young woman with an unusually large and long nose.

PRINCESS GORGONZOLA: (*wailing*) Father! I cannot live with this nose for another minute! I need a new one!

KING: What happened, my dear, to upset you so?

PRINCESS GORGONZOLA: Oh, Father! A child in the garden asked me to move out of the way. He said my nose was blocking the sun!

QUEEN: (*hugging her daughter, who falls weeping into her arms*) Oh, sweetheart!

KING: Ah, my dear Gorgonzola. It may be time, alas, to call in the doctor.

The king nods to one of the servants, who curtsies and walks quickly off stage. The servant returns with Doctor Snozzarello. The doctor is a handsome young man whose nose is even larger and longer than Princess Gorgonzola's.

DOCTOR SNOZZARELLO: (*bowing*) Doctor Snozzarello, plastic surgeon, at your service. (*standing*) And where is the patient?

PRINCESS GORGONZOLA: (*standing apart from her mother and wiping tears from her eyes*) It is I.

Doctor Snozzarello gasps.

DOCTOR SNOZZARELLO: (*speaking in a booming voice and clapping his hands*) Everyone! Please clear the room! Except for the princess! (*looking at the king and queen*) Even Your Highnesses, please.

Everyone clears the stage, except for Princess Gorgonzola and Doctor Snozzarella. He examines her face.

DOCTOR SNOZZARELLO: Your Highness, you cannot truly wish me to change one thing about this perfect masterpiece!

PRINCESS GORGONZOLA: Masterpiece? With this nose? (*beginning to weep again*) I want a small nose, not this giant one . . . (*in a lower voice*) . . . a nose that Dashing Derek could love.

DOCTOR SNOZZARELLO: Dashing Derek cannot love you just as you are? Is Dashing Derek himself without a <u>flaw</u>? Very well. We shall schedule the operation, but for next week. Perhaps between now and then you will change your mind—or heart.

Scene 2

The next morning, a picnic at the palace. Downstage left, Doctor Snozzarello sits on a blanket, entertaining some children with a finger puppet. Dashing Derek walks on stage with two ladies clinging to each arm. Princess Gorgonzola enters from the opposite side.

PALACE LADIES: Oh, Derek, please join us in the archery competition!

DASHING DEREK: Ladies! Ladies! Ah, no, I do not plan to compete for the silver cup. However, if any of you happens to win the cup, I'll gladly accept it. In the meantime, I'll sit right here. (*With a flourish, Dashing Derek sits on a blanket downstage right.*)

PRINCESS GORGONZOLA: (*in a low voice, to herself*) Then I shall have to win the silver cup!

Each of the ladies does her best in the archery competition. Princess Gorgonzola's turn is last. Her arrow flies straight into the bull's-eye! The silver cup is hers!

After a page gives her the cup, Princess Gorgonzola walks with it toward Dashing Derek—and then stops short. Derek is lounging on his blanket, admiring his own reflection in a water glass. She stares at him for a moment, frowning. Then she turns toward Doctor Snozzarello. The children laugh at his finger puppet—and so does Princess Gorgonzola. She marches toward him and hands him the cup.

PRINCESS GORGONZOLA: The silver cup—please, it is yours!

DOCTOR SNOZZARELLO: (*handing the cup back to her*) Oh, no, Your Highness. The cup is yours. You won it on your own. Just as you have won . . . (*bowing*) If I may be bold enough to say it—just as you have won my heart.

PRINCESS GORGONZOLA: (*giving her hand to the doctor*) Just as I am, Doctor?

DOCTOR SNOZZARELLO: (*taking her hand and kissing it*) Yes, just as you are, Your Highness!

7. How is information about the actions of the characters given in "Problem in the Palace"?

   A. through description

   B. through dialogue

   C. through stage directions

   D. through illustrations

8. Why do the king and queen want all the mirrors covered at the beginning of the play?

   A. They believe the princess is ugly.

   B. They do not want the mirrors to break.

   C. They want the princess to forget about her nose.

   D. They think that the mirrors are bad luck.

9. Which word means the OPPOSITE of <u>flaw</u>?

   A. fault

   B. heart

   C. opinion

   D. perfection

10. Which word BEST describes Dashing Derek?

   A. vain

   B. tired

   C. greedy

   D. competitive

11. How is Doctor Snozzarello different from Dashing Derek?

   A. He is ugly.

   B. He enjoys archery.

   C. He cares about others.

   D. He wants the silver cup.

12. What is the theme of this play? Give an example from the play that shows this theme.

   _____

   _____

   _____

   _____

   _____

Speed Demons with Wings

The pilot couldn't believe his eyes. He was diving his plane at 170 miles per hour when a bird hurtled down past his window. The pilot later told a newspaper reporter that it was "as though the plane was standing still."

It was business as usual for this remarkable bird, a peregrine falcon. It was simply diving to catch its dinner, scooping a duck right out of the air just as you might scoop a spoonful of peas off your plate.

Swift Hunter on High

The peregrine falcon is a sleek bird about the size of a crow. Its flying and hunting skills are legendary. With its large eyes and sharp eyesight, a peregrine spots prey flying far below. Then it folds in its mighty wings and dives through the air at speeds up to two hundred miles per hour! The unlucky prey doesn't have much chance of escaping this speed demon.

Like all birds of prey, the peregrine has powerful feet with strong <u>talons</u> that enable it to catch, carry, and tear apart its prey. It hunts from high above the ground by cruising through the upper air or peering down from a towering perch. When it spots its prey, the peregrine dives at full speed and hits its prey with its foot. At such a high speed, the blow may kill the prey immediately, or at least stun it into confusion. And if the peregrine doesn't hit its target on the dive down, it will try to strike from below on the way up again! When it hits, the peregrine swoops back to see if it can catch and eat its prey in midair. But if the bird is too large or heavy, then the falcon will let it fall and eat it down on the ground.

Peregrines can be found in many parts of the world. Usually they nest on high cliffs, but some can be found on skyscrapers or bridges. Peregrines are not picky about their habitat. They usually do well in any moderate climate with a steady supply of food.

Swift Runner of the Plains

Another speedy bird spends its entire life on the ground. The ostrich lives in the plains and deserts of Africa. Its large, shaggy wings are not for flying. Instead, the bird uses them for show and to help it balance itself as it runs. And it can *really* run. A full-grown ostrich is able to sprint in short bursts at speeds of about forty miles per hour.

What makes its great speed more amazing is that the ostrich is not small and sleek like the peregrine falcon. It is the largest and heaviest of all birds, standing as tall as nine feet and weighing as much as 345 pounds. How can this enormous bird be the fastest two-legged animal on Earth? Because the ostrich's muscular legs have unusually long, elastic tendons. Tendons connect muscle to bone, and the ostrich's act like springs, powering the bird forward. Even as the ostrich races along, its head always stays level. All the action takes place in its mighty legs and two-toed feet.

The Swiftest of Them All

The forty-mile-per-hour sprints of the ostrich might not seem so impressive when compared with the two hundred-mile-per-hour dives of the peregrine falcon. Remember, though, that the ostrich achieves its speed through the power of its legs. The peregrine, on the other hand, dives with the help of gravity.

What bird flies the fastest through the power of its own wings? That title just might go to the little bird called the swift. One type of swift, the white-throated needletail, has been reported as flying as fast as 105 miles per hour. This record cannot be verified, however. The needletail's relative, the common swift, has accurately been recorded as flying on its own at seventy miles per hour. That's as fast as the cheetah runs!

Animal Speeds	
Animal	**Top Speed (mph)**
Human	28
Greyhound	39
Ostrich	40
Race horse	48
Hummingbird	60
Sailfish	65
Cheetah	70
Common swift	70
Peregrine falcon	200

13. Which word means about the same as <u>talons</u> as it is used in this passage?

  A. claws

  B. fingers

  C. wings

  D. feathers

14. According to the passage, why is the peregrine falcon MOST LIKELY to kill its prey immediately when it hits it with its feet?

  A. The peregrine's feet are especially strong.

  B. The peregrine's speed is deadly to its prey.

  C. The peregrine's eyesight gives it good aim.

  D. The peregrine's wings are powerful.

15. The swift MOST LIKELY got its name because of its

  A. size.

  B. song.

  C. speed.

  D. strength.

16. According to the chart, which is MOST LIKELY the fastest animal in the water?

  A. human

  B. sailfish

  C. cheetah

  D. peregrine falcon

17. According to the chart, which animal runs faster than a human but slower than an ostrich?

    A. greyhound

    B. race horse

    C. cheetah

    D. peregrine falcon

18. Using information from the passage, explain how the ostrich is able to run so fast.

    _____

    _____

    _____

    _____

    _____

It's a Blast!

At 8:32 on a Sunday morning in March 2000, the Seattle Kingdome collapsed to the ground in a billowing cloud of dust. The sports arena had been built to last. But when the city decided to tear it down, it was gone in less than seventeen seconds. Who could turn more than one hundred thousand tons of steel and concrete into a pile of rubble in just a few blinks of the eye?

To knock down a brick wall, you might use a sledgehammer. To knock down a small building, you might use a wrecking ball. To demolish something really big, like a skyscraper, bridge, or massive sports arena, you'll definitely need a specialist: an imploder!

A Dynamite Job

Imploders don't just stick dynamite into a building. In fact, they often plan for months before a sixteen-second implosion! The first thing they do is examine the structure that's coming down. They look for the main support columns of the building. They place the explosives on these columns, because once the support of a building is gone, gravity will do the rest of the work. It's the same thing that happens when a person gets tackled in the legs: without support, there is nowhere to go but down.

Imploders don't actually blow things up; they let things fall down. Therefore, they have to figure out in which direction a structure should fall. Imagine a table with two legs broken on one side: It will topple down on that side. Falling to one side might be OK for a grain silo standing in the middle of an empty field, but not for a skyscraper in the middle of a crowded city street. Luckily, imploders can control which way a building will fall by deciding *where* to put the explosives and *when* to detonate, or explode, them. The explosion doesn't always happen in one "big bang." Many times the explosives are set off in several smaller stages.

Safety First

If you lived next to a building that was going to be demolished, you'd probably have many questions about your safety. Safety is the most important thing to demolition experts, too. Long before demolition day, they talk to people who work or live near the site. They tell the people about other demolitions and let them know what to expect in their neighborhood on demolition day. Will the windows in their building shatter? Will the foundation crack? Will the implosion make the ground shift? Specialists who study ground and air vibrations are hired during the planning stages to answer these questions for people. Usually their answer is "no."

As demolition day gets closer, crews are hired to remove fixtures and nonsupporting walls from the building. This way, flying debris is less likely to hurt people or damage surrounding buildings during the implosion. It also makes the pile of rubble easier to clean up after it's all over.

Ready, Set, Charge!

It's early Sunday morning, and the building is almost ready. Holes for the explosives are bored into the support columns. Concrete shafts are wrapped in special fabric to catch flying debris. Windows of nearby buildings are covered with protective material. Finally, the explosives can be loaded. Yards of wire are snaked from the building to the detonator. A barrier fence goes up. No one is allowed inside the area once the explosives are in place.

After the area is cleared, the blasters get ready at the electrical detonator controls. The countdown begins, and warning sirens may blare. The blaster presses the "charge" button that allows an electrical charge to build up. When the light comes on showing that the charge is ready—and the countdown is complete—he pushes the "fire" button. Suddenly, the built-up electrical charge is released into the wires, and almost magically, the majestic building starts to crumble to the ground.

19. When planning for a demolition, which do imploders and their crews do FIRST?

A. remove fixtures and nonsupporting walls

B. put up a barrier fence to keep people away

C. find the main support columns of the building

D. wrap concrete shafts with special fabric

20. Read this sentence from the passage.

Imploders don't actually blow things up; they let things fall down.

Based on this sentence, you can conclude that an implosion is the OPPOSITE of

A. an explosion.

B. a displosion.

C. a building.

D. a climb.

21. Read this sentence from the passage.

Falling to one side might be OK for a grain silo standing in the middle of an empty field, but not for a skyscraper in the middle of a crowded city street.

What can you infer would happen if a skyscraper fell to one side?

A. Imploders would not be able to destroy it.

B. It would be likely to fall on top of something.

C. The explosives would not detonate.

D. The foundations of nearby buildings would crack.

22. Which text structure is used in the section titled "Safety First"?

A. cause and effect

B. problem and solution

C. compare and contrast

D. chronological order

23. Which is the BEST summary of this passage?

A. The Seattle Kingdome was built to last, but it was destroyed in less than seventeen seconds due to the careful planning of imploders.

B. Whereas demolishing a brick wall requires a sledgehammer, and a small building a wrecking ball, demolishing a large building requires an imploder.

C. An implosion that happens in seconds takes months of planning by specialists who think about how the building should fall and how to keep people safe while it falls.

D. Imploders don't just stick dynamite into a building or even blow it up; they just plan carefully until it falls down.

24. The author writes that "safety is the most important thing to demolition experts." Give two examples from the passage that show that safety is important to demolition experts.

_____

_____

_____

_____

Part 2: Language Arts

This passage contains mistakes. Read the passage and answer the questions that follow.

Tornado

(1) It was a cloudy day. (2) Papa, and I were working in the fields again. (3) We plowed the uneven ground and planted our summer crops. (4) Then he showed me how to repair a broken fence. (5) By late afternoon I was grumpy, hot, and tired. (6) "Papa," I sighed. (7) "Life here is difficult. (8) I'm not sure I like being a pioneer. (9) I miss living in the city."

(10) Papa stopped working, and looked at me. (11) "Remember, Jacob," Papa said, "we have lived in Kansas for only a year. (12) The first year is the hardest. (13) When things get a little easier, you may have a change of heart."

(14) Suddenly, the sky turned dark gray. (15) It was early in the afternoon, but the day grew dark as night. (16) We heard a loud roar, and a strong wind whipped at us. (17) Then we saw the huge funnel cloud. (18) It could mean only one thing. (19) "Tornado! Hurry!" yelled Papa.

(20) Mama, Sarah, and Carmine ran from the barn where they had been milking the cows. (21) We all ran to the root cellar in the back of the house.

(22) Papa had built the root cellar to store our fruits and vegetables. (23) But he also made it large enough so that we could use it for a storm shelter. (24) After we climbed down the ladder, Papa bolted the wooden door. (25) We sat on the cool, damp floor. (26) A noise like a hundred screaming freight trains rumbled overhead. (27) The door jiggled, but it did not blow open. (28) We were safe, but scared.

(29) "We'll stay here until the twister has passed and I'm sure it's not dangerous to go outside," Papa said. (30) "It may be a while."

(31) Sarah said, "I wish it were a sunny day. (32) Then we could go on a picnic."

(33) "After we ate, we could go swimming in the creek," Carmine added. (34) "We never went swimming when we lived in the city."

(35) "Then we could take the long way home," Mama said. (36) "We'd walk right past the blackberry vines and pick enough to make a pie for dinner."

(37) Papa said, "After dinner we could read a book together."

(38) Listening to my family talk about our life in the country, I realized that I enjoy life here. (39) I'd even forgotten for a moment about the tornado blowing over our land. (40) "I'm glad we moved here" I said.

(41) At last, it was quiet outside. (42) We all smiled and gave each other quick hugs. (43) Then Papa reached up to open the cellar door.

25. Which of the following sentences is punctuated correctly?

    A. Papa, and I were working in the fields again.

    B. Papa stopped working, and looked at me.

    C. It was early in the afternoon, but the day grew dark as night.

    D. We were safe, but scared.

26. Read sentence 20 from the passage.

    Mama, Sarah, and Carmine ran from the barn where they had been milking the cows.

    Which of the following correctly identifies the dependent clause and underlines the relative adverb?

    A. <u>from</u> the barn

    B. <u>where</u> they had been milking the cows

    C. they <u>had been milking</u>

    D. Mama, Sarah, and Carmine <u>ran from the barn</u>

27. Read sentence 16 from the passage.

    We heard a loud roar, and a strong wind whipped at us.

    Which is the BEST way to rewrite sentence 16?

    A. We heard a loud roar, and a strong wind whipped on us.

    B. We heard a loud roar, and a strong wind whipped around us.

    C. We heard a loud roar, and a strong wind whipped down us.

    D. We heard a loud roar, and a strong wind whipped in us.

28. Read sentence 38 from the passage.

    Listening to my family talk about our life in the country, I realized that I enjoy life here.

    Which is a way to write this sentence to show that Jacob began to have fun in the past and continues to have fun now?

    A. Listening to my family talk about our life in the country, I realized that I will enjoy life here.

    B. Listening to my family talk about our life in the country, I realized that I had enjoyed life here.

    C. Listening to my family talk about our life in the country, I realized that I am going to enjoy life here.

    D. Listening to my family talk about our life in the country, I realized that I have been enjoying life here.

29. Read sentence 40 from the passage.

"I'm glad we moved here" I said.

Which is the BEST way to punctuate sentence 40?

A. "I'm glad, we moved here" I said.

B. "I'm glad we moved, here" I said.

C. "I'm glad we moved here," I said.

D. "I'm glad we moved here", I said.

30. Read sentences 17 and 18 from the passage.

Then we saw the huge funnel cloud. It could mean only one thing.

Rewrite these sentences using the relative pronoun *that* to join them into one sentence.

_____

_____

_____

Part 3: Writing

Opinion Piece Prompt

Your school board wants to redesign the school calendar. One option is to have year-round schooling with four three-week breaks, one during each season. The other option is to have a traditional calendar that includes the eight-week summer break and one-week breaks in December, February, and April. Write a persuasive essay to the school board telling them which option you think is best. Use reasons and examples to support your response.

Use the checklist below to help you do your best writing.

Does your opinion piece

❏ introduce a topic and state an opinion on that topic?

❏ group related ideas in an organized structure?

❏ include reasons that are supported by facts and details?

❏ use transitional words and phrases to help readers follow your opinion and reasons?

❏ use a style and vocabulary that make sense for the audience and purpose?

❏ have a conclusion that sums up your opinion?

❏ use good spelling, capitalization, and punctuation?

❏ follow the rules for good grammar?

Use the following pages to plan and write your response.

Planning Page

Summative Assessment

Read the passage and answer the questions that follow.

Mauna Loa: Long Mountain

It was a warm, humid evening in Hawaii in 1855. An American named Titus Coan was observing the volcano Mauna Loa. As he stood near the mountain he noticed a small point of light at its peak. At first the light looked like a bright star. Before long, however, the night sky began to glow as if it were morning. He soon realized that the glow was caused by the hot, molten rock called lava. Mauna Loa was erupting!

What's Special about Mauna Loa?

The 1855 eruption continued for fifteen months! Since an eruption in 1843 (also witnessed by Titus Coan), Mauna Loa has erupted thirty-three times. The most recent eruption was in 1984 and lasted for three weeks.

Each time Mauna Loa erupts, the lava that flows down its sides hardens into new rock, adding height and width to the mountain. After centuries of eruptions, Mauna Loa is about sixty miles long and thirty miles wide. Its name, in fact, means "Long Mountain." A volcano formed by lava flows is called a shield volcano. That's because the mountain looks like a warrior's shield.

Did you know that Mauna Loa is taller than Mount Everest? Mount Everest rises approximately 29,000 feet (8.8 km) above sea level. However, Mauna Loa's base is below sea level, on the ocean floor. Not only that, but the mountain's own weight has pushed the ocean floor down an additional 26,000 feet. Measured from its undersea base to its summit, Mauna Loa is about 56,080 feet (17.1 km) tall!

What's It Like to Have a Volcano for a Neighbor?

The people of Hawaii live with Mauna Loa and other volcanoes all their lives. But it is not easy because a volcanic eruption is powerful, unstoppable, and even deadly. As Mike Rhodes, a scientist who studies Mauna Loa, says, "The sound and the vibration [or shaking] take over your body. . . . There's the intense heat. There's the smell of the gases that makes you choke and makes your eyes water. And there's always a sense of excitement, bordering on fear."

Today, Mauna Loa is part of Hawai'i Volcanoes National Park. Scientists there carefully monitor the volcanoes. Hikers have to check in with park rangers before they go out on a trail, and they must check in again when they return.

How Do the Facts Relate to the Myth?

Scientists have discovered that the Hawaiian Islands are not all the same age. The most western island, Kauai, is the oldest. From west to east, each island is older than the next. There are a few underground zones on Earth where molten rock is always very close to the surface. These zones are called "hot spots." There is a "hot spot" at the eastern end of the Hawaiian Islands. Right over it is Hawaii, the youngest island. There, Mauna Loa and the other active volcanoes are found. Volcanoes on the other, older islands are extinct. They no longer erupt.

The ancient Hawaiian myth about Pele, the volcano goddess, is based on these facts. According to the myth, Pele and her sister have a big fight. Pele is forced to move. She arrived first at Kauai and made a volcano. Her sister then filled it with seawater to put it out. From there, Pele traveled eastward, making volcanoes as she went from island to island. Her sister put out each volcano. Afterward, Pele settled in the crater of Kilauea, the most active volcano on Hawaii. Whenever the hot-tempered Pele gets upset, she causes lava to flow and the ground to shake.

How Do People Feel about Mauna Loa?

The people who live in the shadow of Mauna Loa worry about protecting themselves from future eruptions of the volcano. However, they can feel safe knowing that scientists continue to study Mauna Loa and watch for its next eruption.

1. Which detail from the section titled "What's Special about Mauna Loa?" BEST supports the idea that Mauna Loa is special?

   A. Mauna Loa has erupted thirty-three times since 1843.

   B. *Mauna Loa* means "Long Mountain."

   C. Mauna Loa is a type of volcano called a shield volcano.

   D. Mauna Loa is actually taller than Mount Everest.

2. How does Mike Rhodes, the scientist, feel about volcanic eruptions?

   A. They are disgusting.

   B. They are thrilling.

   C. They are terrifying.

   D. They are mostly safe.

3. At Hawai'i Volcanoes National Park, what is MOST LIKELY the reason hikers need to check in with park rangers both before they go out on a trail and when they return?

   A. The rangers want to know who is out on the trails if there is an eruption.

   B. The rangers want to be sure that the hikers do not fall into a "hot spot."

   C. Hikers at this park tend to be less responsible than those at other parks.

   D. Hikers at this park are likely to encounter bears and other wild animals.

4. According to the passage, why are the active volcanoes of the Hawaiian Islands found to the east?

   A. Molten rock is close to the surface there.

   B. The islands are older there.

   C. The climate is warmer there.

   D. Sunlight is more direct there.

5. Which is the BEST summary of the story of Pele?

    A. Pele made a volcano on Kauai, but her sister filled it with seawater to put it out, so Pele traveled eastward.

    B. Pele is said to live in the crater of Kilauea, and whenever she gets upset, the volcano erupts.

    C. Pele made the volcanoes of Hawaii, which her sister put out, until she finally settled in the crater of Kilauea.

    D. Pele traveled eastward, making the volcanoes of Hawaii, until she had a big argument with her sister.

6. In what ways does the myth about Pele relate to the facts about the Hawaiian Islands? Give two examples from the passage.

_____

_____

_____

_____

_____

Read the story and answer the questions that follow.

A Daring Rescue

Uncle Jerry and I plodded through the muddy water and high winds. A tropical storm warning had been issued, and we were going to check on our neighbor, Mr. Haley. When we finally reached his house, the water had risen so high that the first step was <u>submerged</u>.

Uncle Jerry banged on the front door. All we could hear was Mr. Haley's dog, Duke, barking in the distance. Uncle Jerry yelled out Mr. Haley's name, but only Duke responded. Uncle Jerry opened up the unlocked front door, and we followed the barking to the back of the house. When Uncle Jerry swung open the door to the back porch, Duke's frantic greeting almost knocked us down. "Calm down, boy," said Uncle Jerry. "What's going on, Duke? Where's Mr. Haley?"

That's when we heard a weak voice coming from the corner of the porch. "I sure did it this time, didn't I?"

We turned our flashlights toward the voice. There beneath a window was Mr. Haley, curled on his side, with a ladder lying next to him. "I think I busted my leg," he explained, shivering in the cold.

After wrapping Mr. Haley in a blanket, Uncle Jerry turned to me. "He won't be able to wade through the water, and I can't carry him all that way. I'm going to stay here with him, so I need you to go back to the car and unhitch the johnboat. It needs only a foot of water to float, so you can guide it right up to the front porch. We'll load Mr. Haley into the boat, ferry him to the car, and drive him to the hospital."

With these instructions, I stepped off the porch into what used to be the backyard and what was now becoming a raging river. "C'mon, Nick," I said to myself. "Don't mess this one up. Mr. Haley is counting on you!"

Rain pelted my face. I could hardly see anything as I made my way against the rushing water. Then, when my jacket caught on a tree branch, I dropped my flashlight into the water. The darkness seemed to swallow me.

Just as I was about to panic, I thought I heard something. I threw back the hood of my slicker to listen. Then I heard it again—a car horn blaring not far from where I stood. It was Aunt Jan!

She jumped out of Uncle Jerry's car. "What's wrong, Nick? Where is everyone?" Once I explained what had happened, Aunt Jan returned to the car and backed it into the flooded yard as far as she dared. I pushed the johnboat off its trailer and found that Uncle Jerry had been right: The boat had no trouble staying afloat. We tied a line to the front of the boat, and I led the way toward the house. Aunt Jan held up her flashlight, but I could see only the trees and water directly in front of me. If I missed the house, we could end up in the swollen creek behind it. But then, I had an idea.

"Hey, Duke!" I yelled at the top of my lungs. Aunt Jan caught on right away and joined in. Together we shouted Duke's name over and over into the storm. Every time he heard us, Duke started barking. Every time Duke stopped barking, we called out his name again. We guided the boat toward him through the water, and before long, we were on the front porch.

Uncle Jerry was relieved. We helped him carry Mr. Haley to the front porch, but getting him into the boat was tricky. After we lifted Duke into the boat, it was finally time to head out for the road again. Uncle Jerry told me to take the lead, and this time, I charged ahead with confidence back toward the car.

7. Why is the setting important to the story?

    A. It causes Nick to get lost.

    B. It explains why Duke barks so much.

    C. It creates problems for the characters.

    D. It results in Mr. Haley's being unprepared for a flood.

8. Which word means the same as <u>submerged</u> as it is used in this story?

    A. wet

    B. steep

    C. broken

    D. underwater

9. Why do Nick and Aunt Jan yell Duke's name?

    A. to help them locate Mr. Haley's house

    B. to let Uncle Jerry know they are coming

    C. to keep themselves from getting afraid

    D. to make sure the dog does not bother Uncle Jerry

10. Which word BEST describes the main character, Nick?

    A. resourceful

    B. frightened

    C. careless

    D. clumsy

11. Which sentence BEST states the theme of this story?

    A. It is best not to take risks during a flood.

    B. Dogs are the best friends a person can have.

    C. Thinking creatively can help in times of trouble.

    D. Getting involved with neighbors just causes problems.

12. Why does Nick feel confident when he returns to the car at the end of the story? Give at least one reason why he would feel more confident after the events in this story.

_____

_____

_____

_____

Read the poem and answer the questions that follow.

The Andes

South America has the Andes, colossal and proud—
Their craggy shoulders straight, and their heads in the clouds.
Like snowy giants, the mountains touch the skies;
They are rugged lions gazing with fearless, heartless eyes.

5   In the central Andes, volcanoes can be found.
Hot and fiery, they explode from the ground.
This is how newborn mountains grow
When volcanoes erupt like a fireworks show.

In the central Andes, temperatures are mild
10   And there the forests remain wild.
Among the lofty trees, proud bears roam,
And mysterious cats stake empty caves as home.

In the north, the Andes change from wet to dry;
Above the mountains, enormous birds fly.
15   A parade of animals ambles through—
The muddy Amazon River begins life here, too.

Across the Andes, Earth declares another day done;
Wild animals sleep, as does the sun.
Above the frosty peaks, a shimmering star appears
20   Glittering like a diamond as the cool night sky clears.

13. Which statement about the rhymes in each stanza is true?

    A. Only lines 3 and 4 rhyme.

    B. Lines 1 and 2 rhyme, and lines 3 and 4 rhyme.

    C. Lines 1 and 3 rhyme, and lines 2 and 4 rhyme.

    D. Lines 1 and 4 rhyme, and lines 2 and 3 rhyme.

14. In the first stanza, the Andes are described as having "craggy shoulders" and "heads in the clouds" as part of a simile comparing them to

    A. South America.

    B. giants.

    C. lions.

    D. eyes.

15. Which version shows which syllables are stressed in line 5?

    A. In the <u>central</u> <u>An</u>des, vol<u>ca</u>noes <u>can</u> be <u>found</u>.

    B. <u>In</u> the <u>central</u> <u>An</u>des, <u>vol</u>canoes can <u>be</u> found.

    C. <u>In</u> the <u>central</u> Andes, vol<u>ca</u>noes <u>can</u> <u>be</u> <u>found</u>.

    D. In the <u>central</u> An<u>des</u>, vol<u>ca</u>noes <u>can</u> be <u>found</u>.

16. How are the northern Andes different from the central Andes?

    A. The mountains are taller.

    B. The climate is drier.

    C. The birds are larger.

    D. Animals live there.

17. What is this poem MOSTLY about?

    A. the beauty of the Andes

    B. how the Andes came to be

    C. the different animal species of the Andes

    D. the weather in different parts of the Andes

18. What does the metaphor comparing the Andes to "rugged lions" tell about the mountains?

    _____

    _____

    _____

    _____

    _____

Read the passage and answer the questions that follow.

The Lewis and Clark Expedition

In May 1803, the United States bought the Louisiana Territory from France. This territory was much larger than today's state of Louisiana. In fact, it was so large that its purchase doubled the size of the country! However, even the diplomats who made the deal with the French did not know where the boundaries of the new territory were.

Luckily, just a few months earlier, Congress had given President Thomas Jefferson money for an <u>expedition</u> along the Missouri River and to the Pacific Ocean. President Jefferson wanted to increase the area where American fur traders could work. Now, the expedition could also find out more about the United States' new territory.

The man President Jefferson chose to lead the expedition was Meriwether Lewis, his private secretary. Lewis then asked William Clark to lead the expedition with him. They had served together in the U.S. Army. By December 1803, they settled in Camp River Dubois in Illinois, near St. Louis, Missouri, with a group of about thirty men. After several months of training, in May 1804 the group was ready to go.

The Trip to the Pacific

In its first five months, the expedition made its way up the Missouri River as far as the site where Bismarck, North Dakota, is today. There they built Fort Mandan and settled for the winter. Through the winter months, Lewis and Clark prepared maps, papers, and samples of plants, minerals, and other objects. In the following April, about fifteen or sixteen members of the expedition took these materials back to St. Louis. The rest of the group continued up the Missouri River.

During the summer of 1805, the Lewis and Clark expedition traveled through lands that nonnatives had never seen before. To help them, they hired two translators: a French Canadian trader, Toussaint Charbonneau, and his Shoshoni wife, Sacagawea. Lewis was especially grateful to have the help of the Shoshoni when he first saw the Rocky Mountains. "I discovered immence [very large] ranges of high mountains still to the west of us with their tops partially covered with snow," he wrote. But a group of Shoshoni led by Sacagawea's brother Cameahwait sold horses to the expedition and also provided a guide. They made their way safely across the Rockies. Three months later, on November 15, 1805, they arrived at the Pacific Ocean. "Ocean in view!" wrote Clark in his journal. "O! The joy!"

Accomplishments of the Expedition

By the time the expedition returned to St. Louis in September 1806, the group had done many of the things that President Jefferson had hoped they would do. They had failed to do only one thing: find an all-water route to the Pacific Ocean. Of course, there was no way they could have succeeded at that task, because such a route does not exist! Nevertheless, Lewis and Clark had gone all the way to the Pacific Ocean. They had taken detailed notes about what they saw or whom they met along the way, including plants, animals, and various groups of Native Americans. Lewis identified 178 plants and 122 animals that were unknown to Western science, including the grizzly bear and prairie dog. The group also established good relations with many Native American groups. As a result, the American fur trade expanded to the West. Also, more explorers followed Lewis and Clark, opening the West to American settlers.

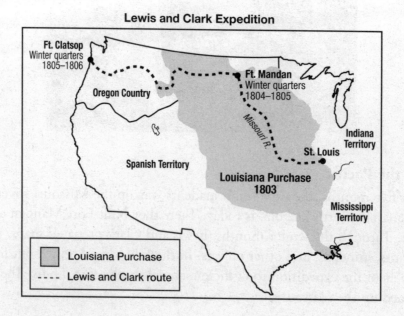

Lewis and Clark Expedition

19. The Latin root *ped-* means "foot." Which tells what <u>expedition</u> means as it is used in this passage?

A. a list of discoveries

B. a trip taken for a purpose

C. a slow walk through the woods

D. a path taken across the mountains

20. Which detail from the passage BEST supports the idea that the purchase of Louisiana Territory gave another reason for an expedition across the west?

A. The United States doubled in size with the purchase of Louisiana Territory.

B. The United States did not know where the boundaries of its new territory were.

C. President Jefferson wanted American fur traders to be able to work in a larger area.

D. President Jefferson had already gotten the money needed for an expedition across the west.

21. What is the MOST LIKELY reason that Meriwether Lewis was grateful for the help of the Shoshoni in crossing the Rocky Mountains?

A. The mountains were surprisingly large.

B. Members of the expedition had never seen snow before.

C. No one but the Shoshoni knew that the mountains existed.

D. Knowledge of the Shoshoni language was needed to cross the mountains.

22. Read this statement from the passage.

"Ocean in view!" wrote Clark in his journal. "O! The joy!"

How does the viewpoint in this statement differ from the viewpoint in the rest of the passage?

A. It explains that the expedition was finally over.

B. It tells why Lewis and Clark never found an all-water route to the Pacific.

C. It expresses a strong feeling.

D. It shows a positive view of Lewis and Clark.

23. Which of the following questions is answered in this passage?

   A. What was the purpose of the Lewis and Clark expedition?

   B. Where did American fur traders work before the expedition?

   C. How many miles did the Lewis and Clark expedition travel?

   D. How did Lewis and Clark get back to St. Louis from the Pacific?

24. For what reasons could the Lewis and Clark expedition be considered successful? Give at least two examples from the passage.

   _____

   _____

   _____

   _____

   _____

Part 2: Language Arts

This passage contains mistakes. Read the passage and answer the questions that follow.

Halley's Comet

(1) What are your plans for July 28, 2061? (2) That date may be far in the future, but you might want to keep it free. (3) It's the next time Halley's Comet will appear in the night sky. (4) This comet moves past Earth once every seventy-six years. (5) Most people have only one chance in their lifetime to see this amazing site.

(6) When it visits Earth's neighborhood, this comet is usually hard to miss. (7) The comet's bright tail stretches almost halfway across the night sky. (8) In clear weather, people can easily see the comet without using a telescope.

(9) In fact, people first wrote about Halley's Comet thousands of years ago. (10) The Chinese first described Halley's Comet in 240 BCE. (11) For centuries afterward, people <u>freaked out</u> when they saw it. (12) They thought the comet was a strange and frightening star.

(13) Then, in 1705, Edmond Halley realized that the object people were seeing every seventy-six years was the same comet. (14) That's why Halley's Comet was named after him. (15) He even mapped out the comet's orbit. (16) This helped him figure out when the comet would return.

(17) The orbit that Halley's Comet travels is billions of miles long. (18) Usually, the comet is out in space, far away from the sun. (19) At these times, the comet is quite small and dark. (20) It is cool. (21) As it flies near the sun, the comet grows hot. (22) It sprays out fiery clouds of gas and dust. (23) The clouds form a glowing head and tail. (24) The head can grow ten times as large as Earth. (25) The tail can stretch for millions of miles.

(26) Scientists once guessed that Halley's Comet was round. (27) In 1986, the comet passed by Earth and space probes took pictures of it. (28) These photos proved that the comet wasn't round. (29) Instead, it was shaped more like a peanut. (30) But don't think of this comet as a small thing. (31) The comet is about ten miles long and five miles across. (32) It is huge! (33) Now isn't that worth waiting years and years to see.

25. In which of the following sentences should a comma be added before the word *and*?

A. They thought the comet was a strange and frightening star.

B. At these times, the comet is quite small and dark.

C. In 1986, the comet passed by Earth and space probes took pictures of it.

D. The comet is about 10 miles long and 5 miles across.

26. Read sentence 5 from the passage.

Most people have only one chance in their lifetime to see this amazing site.

Which change should be made to sentence 5?

A. Replace *one* with *won*.

B. Replace *their* with *they're*.

C. Replace *to* with *too*.

D. Replace *site* with *sight*.

27. Which of the following is the MOST formal way of stating the idea expressed by the underlined words in sentence 11?

A. went bonkers

B. would go nuts

C. became scared

D. got a little crazy

28. Read sentences 22 and 23 from the passage.

It sprays out fiery clouds of gas and dust. The clouds form a glowing head and tail.

Which is the BEST way to use a relative pronoun to join sentences 22 and 23?

A. It sprays out fiery clouds of gas and dust forming a glowing head and tail.

B. It sprays out fiery clouds of gas and dust, who form a glowing head and tail.

C. It sprays out fiery clouds of gas and dust, which form a glowing head and tail.

D. It sprays out fiery clouds of gas and dust, whose form a glowing head and tail.

29. Read sentence 33 from the passage.

Now isn't that worth waiting years and years to see.

What is the BEST way to punctuate sentence 33?

A. Now, isn't that worth waiting years and years to see.

B. Now isn't that worth waiting years, and years to see.

C. Now isn't that worth waiting years and years to see!

D. Now isn't that worth waiting years and years to see?

30. Read sentence 15 from the passage.

He even mapped out the comet's orbit.

Rewrite this sentence, adding the adjectives *elliptical* and *long* in the correct order to describe *orbit*.

_____

_____

_____

Part 3: Writing

Read the passages and respond to the prompt that follows.

The San Francisco Earthquake

The following description of the San Francisco earthquake appears in a book by Peter Streets about the history of the city.

One of the most important earthquakes in history lasted barely a minute. It shook the city of San Francisco, California, in the early morning of April 18, 1906. People as far as Oregon to the north and Los Angeles to the south could feel the shaking. The quake caused great damage to the city. For three days after the earthquake itself, fires burned throughout the city. Afterward, the central business district was destroyed. Hundreds of people lost their lives, and more than half of the four hundred thousand people who lived in San Francisco were left homeless.

At the time, people did not know that Earth's surface is divided into several plates. The San Andreas Fault extends from the Gulf of California to San Francisco. At this fault, two plates meet. If the plates slide against each other suddenly, an earthquake results.

In the years since the San Francisco earthquake, geologists have carefully studied the event. These studies have added much to our understanding of how earthquakes work. In fact, studies of this particular earthquake have resulted in the theory of how the shaking of earthquakes is created. As for the city itself, it recovered quickly. The rebuilt version of the city was even grander than the version that the earthquake had destroyed. By the time San Francisco held the Panama-Pacific International Exposition, in 1915, no trace of the disaster remained.

An Eyewitness Account

Jerome B. Clark lived nearby in Berkeley but did business in San Francisco. The earthquake did not hit his home as hard as it did the city, so he left for work as usual that morning. The following is his description of what he saw.

In every direction from the ferry building flames were seething, and as I stood there, a five-story building half a block away fell with a crash, and the flames swept clear across Market Street and caught a new fireproof building recently erected. The streets in places had sunk three or four feet, in others great humps had appeared four or five feet high. The streetcar tracks were bent and twisted out of shape. Electric wires lay in every direction. Streets on all sides were filled with brick and mortar, buildings either completely collapsed or brick fronts had just dropped completely off. Wagons with horses hitched to them, drivers and all, lying on the streets, all dead, struck and killed by the falling bricks, these mostly the wagons of the produce dealers, who do the greater part of their work at that hour of the morning. Warehouses and large wholesale houses of all descriptions either down, or walls bulging, or else twisted, buildings moved bodily two or three feet out of a line and still standing with walls all cracked.

The Call building, a twelve-story skyscraper, stood, and looked all right at first glance, but had moved at the base two feet at one end out into the sidewalk, and the elevators refused to work, all the interior being just twisted out of shape. It afterward burned as I watched it. I worked my way in from the ferry, climbing over piles of brick and mortar and keeping to the center of the street and avoiding live wires that lay around on every side, trying to get to my office. I got within two blocks of it and was stopped by the police on account of falling walls. I saw that the block in which I was located was on fire, and seemed doomed, so turned back and went up into the city.

Not knowing San Francisco, you would not know the various buildings, but fires were blazing in all directions, and all of the finest and best of the office and business buildings were either burning or surrounded. They pumped water from the bay, but the fire was soon too far away from the waterfront to make any efforts in this direction of much avail. The water mains had been broken by the earthquake, and so there was no supply for the fire engines and they were helpless. The only way out of it was to dynamite, and I saw some of the finest and most beautiful buildings in the city, new modern palaces, blown to atoms. First they blew up one or two buildings at a time. Finding that of no avail, they took half a block; that was no use; then they took a block; but in spite of them all the fire kept on spreading.

The City Hall, which, while old, was quite a magnificent building, occupying a large square block of land, was completely wrecked by the earthquake, and to look upon reminded one of the pictures of ancient ruins of Rome or Athens. . . .

Informative Essay Prompt

The author of "The San Francisco Earthquake" says that this earthquake was "one of the most important earthquakes in history." Based on the information in the article, Jerome B. Clark's description, and the photograph of City Hall, explain why the San Francisco earthquake of 1906 was important.

Use the checklist below to help you do your best writing.

Does your informative essay

❑ use information from both the article and Jerome B. Clark's description?

❑ introduce a topic clearly?

❑ use facts, definitions, details, quotations, and examples to develop the topic?

❑ group related information in paragraphs and sections?

❑ use vivid and exact words?

❑ use transitional words and phrases to link your ideas?

❑ use a style and vocabulary that make sense for the audience and purpose?

❑ have a conclusion that sums up your ideas?

❑ use good spelling, capitalization, and punctuation?

❑ follow the rules for good grammar?

Use the following pages to plan and write your response.

Planning Page

Notes

Notes

Notes

Notes

Notes